Climbing Free

Climbing Free

My Life in the Vertical World

Lynn Hill

with Greg Child

Foreword by John Long

 W. W. Norton & Company
New York London

Frontispiece: Negotiating the crux on Calippo in the Dolomites,
Italy (5.13b). (BETH WALD)

For information about permission to reproduce selections from this book, write to
Permissions, W. W. Norton & Company, Inc., 500 Fifth Avenue, New York, NY 10110

Manufacturing by LSC Communications
Book design by Lovedog Studios
Production manager: Julia Druskin

LIBRARY OF CONGRESS CATALOGING-IN-PUBLICATION DATA
Hill, Lynn, 1961–
Climbing free : my life in the vertical world / Lynn Hill
with Greg Child ; foreword by John Long
p. cm.
ISBN 0-393-04981-7
1. Hill, Lynn, 1961–. 2. Women mountaineers—United States—Biography.
3. Mountaineers—United States—Biography. I. Child, Greg. II. Title.
GV199.92.H52 A3 2002
796.52′2′092—dc21 [B]   2002016636
ISBN 0-393-32433-8 pbk.

W. W. Norton & Company, Inc., 500 Fifth Avenue, New York, N.Y. 10110
www.wwnorton.com

W. W. Norton & Company Ltd., 15 Carlisle St, Soho, London W1D 3BS

5 6 7 8 9 0

*To my mother and father,
who took all seven of us on many camping trips across
the country and instilled in me a deep love for and
appreciation of nature.*

*And to those who introduced me to the world of climbing:
my sister Kathy, my brother Bob, and
Chuck Bludworth (1954–1980).*

Contents

Foreword

I first saw Lynn Hill at Trash Can Rock, in Joshua
Tree National Monument, in 1975. She wore a sassy little Grand Prix
driver's hat, gym shorts, a bikini top, and looked about twelve years old
(she was fourteen). Her older brother Bob, and her sister's fiancée,
Chuck, were slip-sliding all over a little slab climb and eventually gave
up. They reluctantly let Lynn tie into the rope and she danced up the
slab in about fifteen seconds. On top, she looked like she'd just been
crowned queen of some exotic land. The boys seemed unimpressed by
her flagrant delight. *Girl's got a future,* I remember thinking.

Maybe three years later, also out at Joshua Tree, John Bachar (at the
time one of the world's greatest free climbers) and I were trying to
scratch up the overhanging side of a ten-foot boulder. Rumor had it
that some Frenchman had climbed it the previous week, but we didn't
believe any such thing, since neither of us could even get started. Then
who should walk around the corner but Lynn Hill. She wasn't a girl

anymore. She smiled, then proceeded to climb straight up that boulder, on her first try. We couldn't have been more amazed had a giraffe pranced by on its front legs. Lynn down-climbed the back side of the boulder and joined us on the front. "That hurt my fingers," she said, not a trace of cunning in her voice. I clasped the first razor-blade holds and still couldn't pull my feet off the ground. Neither could John. I never did climb the damn thing, though not for lack of trying.

Perhaps a year later, Lynn and I were an item and, along with Richard Harrison, were attempting a new climb at Red Rocks, an adventurous sandstone area twenty miles outside Las Vegas, Nevada. Lynn was working up the first pitch, ratcheting up a bottomless chimney that pinched off after about 60 feet, forcing her out onto the steep face to the right. After barely a body length on the face, a hold broke and she was plummeting though the air—and kept plummeting for about 50 feet before a nut finally arrested her fall, leaving her dangling upside down, in midair, about 10 feet off the deck.

"Jesus!" Richard yelled. "You okay?"

I was too stunned to talk. Bar none, that was the most spectacular airball "whipper" we'd ever seen. And a mighty close shave at that. Another 10 feet and she'd have left the cliffside in a black bag.

"I'm fine," she said, slightly annoyed. Straightaway she squeezed back up the chimney, climbed out onto the face, and without hesitation, cranked up to a ledge about 30 feet above.

I mention these anecdotes because they illustrate several traits that remain hallmarks of Lynn's character: enjoyment, excellence without guile, tenacity in fearful situations, and naked boldness. These certainly factored into the success of the five-foot, one-hundred-pound dynamo (and don't believe her if she claims to be bigger) who would soon come to dominate the "greatest sport in the world."

By and large, Lynn Hill was (and still is, when she wants to be) as good as the very best male climbers, which, considering her size, is miraculous. Many climbs favor masculine dimensions, such as wide fist cracks and steep faces obliging a long reach. Lynn comes up to the middle of my chest, and I swear she can slot her fist inside a walnut shell. Yet even on those wide cracks and reachy face climbs she can hold her own. God knows how. On climbs that favor Lynn's stature, especially small hold routes or tricky balance problems, Lynn is untouchable.

Almost from the first days when "Little Lynnie" tied into a rope, the common refrain was, "Who the hell is that girl?!" The macho ones among us—and I marched point for that group—were left to watch and weep as Lynn breezed over what often had cost us several layers of skin and a few of our nine lives. We normally would have growled like wolves at having our male luster dimmed by a woman. But Lynn shattered the gender barrier so thoroughly that no one could put the pieces back together again. So after the initial shock of it all, the bone-deep chauvinism most of us had unconsciously embraced soon melted away like fat off a holiday ham. Guys no longer begged her onto their rope because she was pleasing to the eye, which is reason enough when you're twenty or fifty, but rather because when you tied in with Lynn, you could get up any damn climb. What the hell? Why not cash in while the going's good, meaning so long as you could inveigle Lynn onto the same cord. We all did. Repeatedly. We all wanted our name on a new climb that would stand forever.

Unlike other sports, a climber's deeds are literally fixed in stone. Barring features (such as hand- and footholds) that occasionally break off, a climbing route forever remains the same climbing route, with a difficulty rating arrived at through consensus. Comparing past and present routes, and performances on these routes, is fairly straightforward. The routes Lynn did, many for the first time, remain at the top of anyone's "A" list.

Her greatest triumphs are ghastly hard "free" climbs, a term and deed the lay public often mistakes for "free soloing," which is climbing without a rope. Basically, free climbing is anything using your own body—hands, feet, gams, et al.—for upward progress. Free "routes" are specific paths up given cliffs and usually follow prominent features such as cracks, arêtes, lines of holds or pockets, and so forth. Because severe routes are hit-and-miss even for world-class climbers, falls are frequent and expected. A rope and attending gear are used to safeguard the fall.

When the tackle is used for upward progress, or to hang on to rest after a fall (standard practice), the climber is no longer free climbing, rather "aid" climbing—that is, using the gear as an "aid" to fight gravity. On titanic rock walls, like the blank, overhanging palisades of El Capitan in Yosemite Valley, cracks and features tend to run out—meaning there is nothing for the free climber to clasp—and aid climbing is often the only way up. Here, experienced teams might take a week to scale the 3,000-foot cliffside, slowly, precariously building a ladder of pitons and other gear up the sheer granite ramparts. These two forms, free and aid climbing, are distinctive arts; to Lynn's credit, she excels at both. But it is in her free climbing, often performed on the grandest possible scale, where Lynn Hill made history.

Her first free ascent in 1993 of the Nose route on El Capitan, the most sought-after pure rock climb in the world, remains a high-water mark in a sport where the technical tide rises by the week. It is difficult for a nonclimber to grasp the significance of this effort. Insiders well know how good she was—and still is. But even to authorities in more traditional, media-driven sports, Lynn Hill remains a curiosity who, to my knowledge, has never been contrasted with other great female athletes of her era. Suffice it to say that I am not alone in thinking that throughout the eighties and nineties, Lynn Hill was quite possibly the best female athlete in the world. El Capitan rises in bold testament to this claim.

We all know that "great" men or women are often lousy people, that the Napoleons of the world often advance over the backs of others. We also know how high achievements are often traceable to the love of acclaim. Lynn is the exception to both rules. She would climb anything with most anyone, putting so little emphasis on her stature that it seemed as unreal as watching her walk on water, figuratively speaking. The end result is that many climbers of our era came to call Lynn a close friend, and have the memories to prove it.

Can I take the measure of Lynn's humility and humanity? I won't even try. I trust both will shine through in this engaging book. But in closing, I want to touch on the reasons why I believe Lynn's conquests reach beyond a person scratching up rock walls from Montana to Madagascar.

Mastery is admirable in any field. But when this mastery plays out by slaying gender stereotypes, embracing primal terrors (always a factor in climbing), having the vision and chops to do long-established things in novel ways, fighting through injuries, slim wages, and one's own doubts and insecurities, and growing more modest in the process, a mere rock climb becomes a victory for the human spirit. Through choice or temperament, most of us are followers. Greatness, on the other hand, is almost always a path leading into the unknown and unproven. And Lynn walked that path like a giant.

I have been all over the world and have had the fortune of doing things with many special people, some famous, some anonymous. But the biggest little hero I've ever known is Lynn Hill. The rest of us are just holding her rope.

—John Long
Venice, California
August 2001

Acknowledgments

I started recording anecdotes about my life over
ten years ago, but it took me until now, at the age of forty, to finally
finish writing this book. The story in these pages is by no means a
thorough representation of climbing history, nor even a complete
account of my life. My intent has been to describe the experiences
that have most shaped my life and love for climbing. I've been
extremely fortunate to have had the chance to follow my passion for
climbing for over twenty-six years, and to have been part of such a
wide spectrum of the climbing community across the world. Because
I started climbing in the 1970s, my career bridged the gap between the
great pioneers of previous generations and the sport climbing cham-
pions of today. Although I've seen enormous changes in the sport, I
realize that no matter what generation we are from or what style of
climbing we pursue—from sport climbing to big walls to high-altitude

expeditions—we all share a spirit of adventure, curiosity, and a love of playing in a beautiful natural environment with our friends.

This book would not have happened without the efforts and encouragement of a great many people. I'd like to thank Greg Child, whose superb writing skills and friendship helped make this book a reality. I'd also like to thank my editor, Helen Whybrow, who helped guide me through this entire process, and my agent, Susan Golomb, whose sincere interest and encouragement helped motivate me to carry through to the end.

I would like to express my deepest gratitude to all my friends and family who have listened to me talk about this book for years and who have given me plenty of inspiration and thoughtful advice along the way. The list would be too long to thank everyone, but I'd like to acknowledge the following friends and colleagues: Shaoshana Alexander, John Bachar, Giulia Baciocco, Anna Biller-Collier, Jamie Bludworth, Jim Bridwell, Russ Clune, Ed Connor, Maria Cranor, Pietro Dal Pra, Robyn Erbesfield-Raboutou, Dean Fidelman, Margaret Foster, Brad Fuller, Rolando Garibotti, Mari Gingery, Sallie Greenwood, Linda Gunnerson, Aaron Huey, Steven Kaup, Susan Krawitz, Mike Lechlinski, John Long, Brad Lynch, Roy McClenahan, Jean Milgram, Simon Nadin, Salley Oberlin, Alison Osius, Bob Palais, Russ Raffa, Rick Ridgeway, Mark Robinson, Brooke Sandahl, Isabelle Sandberg, Susan Schwartz, Paul Sibley, Gene and Laura Smith, Antonella Strano, Steve Sutton, Steve Van Meter, Beth Wald, Jean Weiss, Elliot Williams, John and Bridget Winsor, Eva Yablonsky, and all my sponsors who have helped support me in sharing my passion for climbing with others.

I also owe a big thank you to all of the photographers who have generously provided such beautiful images: John Bachar, Thomas Ballenberger, Chris Bonington, Jim Bridwell, Simon Carter, Greg Child, Greg Epperson, Dean Fidelman, Philippe Fragnol, Tom Frost, Oliver Grünewald, Tilmann Hepp, Bob Hill, Mike Hoover, Galen Rowell, Michael Kennedy, John McDonald, Chris Noble, Jessica Perrin-Larrabee, Philippe Poulet, Brian Rennie, Rick Ridgeway, Mark Robinson, Charlie Row, Brooke Sandahl, Marco Scolaris, Sandy Stewart, Pascal Tournaire, Jorge Urioste, Beth Wald, and Heinz Zak.

Climbing Free

Chapter 1

The Perfect Fall

Deep in the countryside of southern France, nestled in a canyon of limestone cliffs the color of soft blue velvet, lies the village of Buoux. It is a sleepy hamlet of old stone-block farmhouses, rambling vineyards, and glades of twisted oaks in which old men and their cherished pigs roam in search of that curiously local delicacy, the truffle. Higher up, on the rocks above the village, are the water-worn ruins of steps, aqueducts, chambers, and battlements, chiseled long ago by medieval cliff dwellers looking for places of refuge during the various religious wars.

The air is quiet at Buoux, save for the grinding song of cicadas or the occasional call of a climber shouting, "Off belay," to a partner on the ground. For Buoux is among the most famous rock climbing destinations in Europe. It is also the place where I almost lost my life.

The day was May 9, 1989, and as I hiked the fifteen-minute walk up the trail to the cliff, I was thinking about my life and how smoothly it seemed to be running. I was twenty-eight years old, an American traveling through France, earning a living as a professional rock climber. I only had to turn my head and look down the hill to see the brand-new car—a compact metallic blue Ford—that I had just won in a climbing competition in Munich, Germany.

It seemed incredible, strange, even a little perverse, that I could win cars and cash and be touted as a star in magazines and on TV for rock climbing—a sport that remained a complete mystery to most people. But I had the knack for winning, consistently, the climbing competitions that were the current rage throughout Europe, and I was ranked as the number one woman in the sport climbing competition circuit. These competitions challenged the contestants to scale an artificial cliff with a difficult course set with adjustable finger and toe grips made of plastic resin that are supposed to simulate the natural features of rock. The contests were held inside sports stadiums, and the walls, lit by floodlights and made of steel scaffolding, plywood, and resin, were shaped like abstract castles. These man-made walls were quite different from the natural cliffs I had learned on, and I found the challenge of competition exhilarating. To be making a living at something that I found so personally gratifying felt too good to be true.

Those were my thoughts that day as I hiked to the base of the cliff with Russ Raffa, my husband of seven months. At the base of the gray-blue wall I dumped my small rucksack on a platform of knotted tree roots and shifted my thinking to the routine of getting ready to climb.

Who knows how many thousands of times I had gone through the motions of launching up from the ground, engaging my fingers and toes with the rock for the hundred feet or so of a route, then clipping my rope into a set of steel "anchors" and being lowered back to the ground by my partner? The routine was as second nature as riding a bicycle or starting a car. It was so intuitive that I barely gave it a thought.

The cliff we were heading toward is called the Styx Wall, after the river in the Hades of Greek mythology over which the souls of the dead must cross. And the name of the route itself was Buffet Froid, which in French means "Cold Buffet." All climbs have a name, and for some quirky reason the climbers who had first ascended this one named it after the cold lunch that is served following a funeral.

Neither of those names registered in my thoughts that day as portents of ill luck, and why should they? It was a cool, blue-skied afternoon, Russ and I had spent a languid morning sleeping in and breakfasting at an auberge—a country inn—back down the winding road that links Buoux to Apt, and Buffet Froid was an easy climb on which we planned to loosen up. Russ decided to lead the first warm-up route of the day. He would set the rope for me from above and I would then "follow" the pitch. A pitch refers to the section of a climb between belay stations, and can be no longer than the length of a rope. In this case, one pitch would get me to the top of the cliff.

Russ prepared to climb. He uncoiled our 165-foot-long climbing rope and lay it in a neat heap on the ground. He buckled his climbing harness around his waist and tied the rope into it. Then he laced up his climbing shoes and finally he left the ground, moving gracefully upward by poising his fingers and toes against ripples and pockets in the rock. Along the way, about every 10 to 15 feet, he passed a steel bolt drilled into the rock.

The idea behind sport climbing is to make a safe path up a cliff so the climber can enjoy the gymnastic play between the human body and steep stone. The bolts on Buffet Froid were outposts of safety, inserted into the rock for climbers to clip their rope into as they passed. The intent of the bolt is not for the climber to use it for aid in getting up the cliff. The bolt is there to catch any accidental falls. So at each bolt, Russ unclipped from his harness a quickdraw—a short sling with a carabiner at either end—and attached it to the bolt. He then clipped the other end of the quickdraw to the rope. Now, if he slipped, he could not fall far beyond that bolt before the rope arrested him.

Standing on the ground, my job as his belayer was to hold the other end of the rope, which was threaded through a small gadget called a belay device. In the event of a fall, my quick reaction and the belay device, which was clipped to my harness, would save the day by pinching the rope tightly and bringing Russ to a stop when his rope came snug against the bolt he had just clipped.

Russ took about ten minutes to climb up Buffet Froid. At the top he came to a pair of immensely strong steel rings, also drilled into the rock. Here he rearranged the system by anchoring himself momentarily, untying from the rope and threading it through the rings. He then tied back into the rope again and let his body weight come onto the rope—and, therefore, onto me—and I lowered him down. Back on the ground he untied and handed me the end of the rope.

"Your turn now, Lynnie," Russ said.

The rope now went up from the ground, where Russ controlled it through his belay device, through the rings at the top of the climb, and back down to me. Thus, for my ascent of Buffet Froid I had the added safety of the rope being above me. Technically, if I fell I would drop barely any distance at all.

During Russ's climb my thoughts had drifted to my next competition, which would be held in Leeds, England. This would be the very first international World Cup contest in which many of the top-ranked men and women climbers would compete. The competition would be fierce. To win, I'd have to be in top mental and physical shape. But these thoughts were like casual mental flotsam. I was relaxed and content—perhaps too much so.

I began by threading the finger-thick nylon strand of rope through my harness with the intention of tying a knot called a bowline, a maritime knot which sailors prize for its strength. But instead of finishing my knot, I decided to walk over to where I left my climbing shoes on the ground about twenty feet away. My shoes happened to be sitting near a Japanese woman who was preparing to climb a route beside Buffet Froid.

"Hi, are you having a good time climbing here in Buoux?" I asked as I laced up my climbing shoes.

"Yes, yes," the Japanese girl had replied, nodding enthusiastically.

When I returned to the base of the climb, I noticed that Russ had already put me on belay. The thought occurred to me that there was something I needed to do before climbing. I asked myself, *Should I take my jacket off?* But I figured since this was a warm-up climb, my jacket wouldn't be a problem, so I dismissed this thought, wiped the dirt off the soles of my shoes, and began climbing.

"Okay, climbing," I said to Russ, using the simple verbal signal all climbers use to tell their partner they are setting off.

But this time the system had a glitch in it: pilot error. I had poked the rope into the loop in my harness, but, distracted by the actions of fetching my rock shoes and chatting with the Japanese girl, I had not tied the knot. The end of the rope hung at my waist, hidden underneath my jacket, like a ticking time bomb. Neither I nor anyone else at the cliff noticed my potentially fatal mistake.

For a confident, expert climber, Buffet Froid poses little challenge. Its rating on the French scale of difficulty is 6b+. On the U.S. scale that's 5.11, which is no pushover, but for a climber used to a diet of 5.13 routes, it's relatively easy. For me, executing its moves would be like a slow warm-up lap in the pool or a gentle bicycle ride over the flats.

I latched on to the first holds, two limestone flakes no wider than matchbooks. Arching my fingers like grappling hooks, I bore my weight onto the flakes, spreading the force across my torso. I then raised a toe up onto a smooth bump on the wall and pressed down with my hands and feet. Lifting myself off the ground, I reached up with my other hand, directing my fingers to a grape-sized pocket denting the wall. I burrowed a fingertip into the hole, shifted my weight onto it, and climbed higher. This basic sequence was repeated foot after foot, yet, I should say, no two moves were alike. That is part of the beauty of

Free climbing in France. (PHILIPPE FRAGNOL)

rock climbing: no two moves are ever the same. That rule applies to all climbs, whether they are easy or hard, because the rock holds infinite variations and possibilities.

At any point in the 72 feet of Buffet Froid's steep face, the rope could have slipped out of my harness and snaked down the cliff through the carabiners to land in a pile on the ground.

It would have been embarrassing to have made such a blunder, but in fact it would have been no big deal to become unattached from the rope while I climbed, because this was a fairly easy climb for me and I knew there was little chance of falling. Sure, the sight of the rope slipping out of my harness and falling down the cliff would have produced a tingling shock wave up my spine. I probably would have had a chance to practice my French by exclaiming, *"Merde!"* Russ would have shouted, "Oh, my God!" and the Japanese girl and other climbers at the cliff would have uttered exclamations in a half dozen languages. But I probably would have solved the problem by either climbing up a few feet or down a few feet, to grab one of the quickdraws clipped to the bolts. I would then have clipped my harness into one of these and hung safely until Russ, who would have found another climber to belay him, climbed up to me with our rope.

But the rope did not detach from my harness and Russ did not get the opportunity to come scampering up the rock to rescue me. Had that happened, we would have engaged in one of those caring-yet-chiding husband-wife tiffs that end in laughter. Doubtless, we'd have retreated down the trail to have a glass of wine in the auberge in the valley. No sense in pushing the odds when the gods of the odds are going against you.

I climbed on.

Over the next five minutes there must have been a dozen more opportunities for the rope to drop from my waist. Only the barest friction of the rope being pressed through a narrow webbing loop on my harness held it in place. It should have fallen out whenever I shifted my weight to the side or whenever Russ pulled down on the rope to take in the slack as I climbed up.

And then I reached the end of the climb, about 72 feet above the ground. That's about the height of a seven-floor apartment building. In front of me were the two steel bolts and the threaded rope: a rig strong enough to hang a car from. To descend safely, I only had to lean back and Russ would hold me, carefully letting the rope slide through his belay device, controlling my speed of descent with his hand. I would descend as if in an elevator and land gently back down on the ground.

Here was the last chance for my mistake to reveal itself before disaster struck. When I yelled to Russ that I had completed the climb, I expected to feel the rope tight against my waist so he could lower me. I glanced down and noticed Russ was talking to someone, so I grabbed the rope with both hands to pull in the slack. I leaned back, expecting the rope to hold me.

Instead, I felt the rush of air against my cheek.

Climbers at the cliff and in the valley that day described a "bloodcurdling scream" that echoed off the walls. My scream—an involuntary shout of horror—was even heard by Pierre, the mayor of Buoux, who sat in the library of his house half a mile away. Looking toward the source of the scream, climbers on neighboring routes saw a figure free-falling down the cliff, carving an outward arc through the sky. All told, I covered the 72 feet in less than two seconds. As fast as that may be, the sight of anyone falling leaves an imprint on a person's memory as sharp as a photographic image etched into a frame of film.

Parachutists talk of the "ground rush effect" in which the rapid approach of the earth getting closer and closer becomes so powerfully mesmerizing that some unfortunate jumpers have forgotten to open their chutes. As I fell backward I waved my arms frantically in a circular motion to keep myself from landing on my head. Instincts dating back to my days as a gymnast must have resurfaced from deep in my subconscious: *Look for a landing,* some inner voice instructed me. I veered toward the leaves of a tree to my left and saw Russ, getting closer, his mouth gaping in confusion and shock. Then I felt the slap of leaves and branches.

It is not true that in a fall one sees one's life flash before one's eyes. There is not enough time for even a single formed thought. But survival instincts are wired on a faster pathway than any other mental process, and when I saw the approaching tree I knew instinctively that my best chance to live was to land in it. If it could be said that I aimed myself at any landing zone, it was toward that short, stunted green oak tree.

Speeding toward it, I tucked my body into a ball, blasted through its branches, then my left buttock slammed into a lattice of tree roots sprawling on the ground. The impact jarred the senses out of me.

Jennifer Cole, an American climber at the cliff that day, said that when I hit I bounced three feet into the air like a rubber ball, then I released my tuck with a flail of arms and smacked onto the ground, face first into the limey dirt.

The next thing I remember was the throb and ring of my brain as my consciousness partially returned. When I opened my eyes, Russ was wiping dirt from my face, my head resting in his lap.

"What happened?" I asked.

"I don't know," replied Russ.

Even if someone had explained that I had not finished tying my knot and had plunged from the top of the cliff, I may not have been able to grasp the meaning of the words. I was stunned, and was now flushed with the unfamiliar processes of shock and injury. I repeated the question.

A crowd of people was forming a circle around me. I heard a mix of languages—English, French, Italian, Polish, Japanese—and I picked up on a conversation about how to get me out of there. Though still in a semi-conscious state, I saw myself more clearly now, and I took stock of my injuries. Most of the pain was in my left arm, which was twisted in an unnatural position. It appeared broken. My jacket was ripped at the chest, and blood leaked through the hole. My butt ached as if a car had hit it.

"What happened?" I repeated. No one seemed to answer.

By now I knew I had done something stupid, and, ridiculously, I felt embarrassed. I stared up at the faces of those huddled around me. Estelle, the mayor's daughter, hovered over me. Her eyes had tears in them and her dark straight hair hung toward me like vines. Russ, still cradling my head, looked ashen. Other climbers seemed to come and go from my field of vision as they scurried back and forth. Already the wheels of a rescue were in motion, but I lay there understanding only one thing: I needed to concentrate on relaxing in order to better cope with the buzzing sensations of pain and confusion.

Sometime around late evening, in a fleeting spell of awareness, I saw that more people had arrived at the cliff: rescue people, dressed in bright orange-colored overalls. I groaned as I felt myself lifted up and placed onto a metal basket-shaped litter. Then I heard the creak of ropes and pulleys as a crew winched me to the top of the Styx Wall, where a helicopter was waiting to airlift me to a hospital more quickly. I saw hands holding the rails of the stretcher, and felt the bump and movement of being carried through some trees and into a field. Finally, there was the din and wind of the chopper, and inside it a rocking sensation that lulled me into a trancelike state.

The next thing I remember clearly was the emergency room in a hospital in Marseilles. Three women in white gowns stood with their backs to me, chatting in French—a language that at the time I could not speak or understand. I began making noises, asking for something for the acute pain in my elbow. But they seemed to ignore me, until all at once they turned around and began cleaning dried blood from my nose and from the thumb-deep stab wound in my pectoral muscle, which a tree root had pierced. Then, just as I was about to complain that I didn't care about a bit of dried blood on my nose, that their attentions were hurting me, I smelled a chemical odor and felt a rush of relief as an opiate shut out the hurt.

Twelve hours later I woke from a dreamless sleep. I lay on my back in a hospital bed. Daylight streamed through the curtained window. Sounds of people moving through the corridor and the mayhem of French traffic on the street outside filtered through the walls. Piece by piece I recollected the events of the previous day. I knew I had fallen from the top of the Styx Wall, though I still was not sure what had gone wrong in a system I considered to be foolproof. Then I saw Russ coming toward me from a corner of the room.

"Thank God you're alive," he said. "You're so lucky. You can't imagine what it was like to see you fall from that high up. I had no idea what happened—I thought you were dead when I turned you over on the ground. You crashed through a small tree, then landed on the ground right between two big boulders. How are you feeling now?"

"I feel like a truck ran over me. What went wrong?"

"I think you forgot to tie your knot."

I felt a sense of embarrassment to have made such a stupid mistake. Ironically, earlier in the week, I had noticed that Russ had forgotten to double-back his harness and I reminded him to do so twice. Then the very next day I forgot to tie my own knot!

It was all coming back to me. I remembered the events leading up to my fall, then the helicopter flight, the nurses in the hospital, and the moment sometime in the dead of night when I had briefly regained consciousness to find myself in a darkened room with my arm dangling over the side of the bed, holding on to a large bucket of water. No sooner did I note this as being odd than the doctor who was standing over me told me to let go of the bucket. At that point my muscles were ready for the next maneuver; the next thing I knew, the doctor took my arm and gave it a sudden tug and a twist. There was a searing pain as the elbow joint slipped back into its correct alignment. Then I had returned to the oblivion of sleep.

My arm now lay propped on a pillow, cradled in a three-quarter-length plaster cast. An IV tube protruded from the other arm and I was lying in a crooked position so as to relieve the pain I felt in my left buttock. Although I was grateful to know that my arm was not broken, only dislocated, still I wondered what permanent nerve or ligament damage I might have suffered. The strength in my arms was my lifeblood; without that power I could not climb. What I could see through the gauze and plaster surrounding my arm was swollen blue flesh. I thought about trying to wriggle my fingers, but there was too much pain and inflammation to even consider it.

As more and more thoughts broke through the haze of the painkiller, I noticed I was seeing through swollen, squinting eyes. Easing myself over the edge of the bed, I held my arm in the cast and shuffled toward the bathroom. When I switched on the light and saw my reflection in the mirror, I let out a groan of revulsion. My eyes were blackened, my cheeks swollen, my hair matted in a clump.

The sight of my beat-up face jarred my thoughts toward reality. I was lucky to be alive, but this would also mean that I would not be competing at the first World Cup competition in the history of the sport.

Disappointment overwhelmed me. I staggered away from the mirror and its ugly reflection. Limping back to my bed, I lay down. How well things had been going until this blunder. I felt I had a good shot at winning the competition in Leeds and I was climbing harder than any woman ever had. Now, so far as I knew, my elbow may never heal well enough to climb at that level again. My life as a competition climber could be over. I'm not the type given to crying, but my eyes grew wet as I realized what I had always known—that nothing in life is guaranteed. Just when everything seems to be going along smoothly, some unexpected crisis always seems to happen.

As I stared at the white ceiling, my mind filled with the kind of questions that come up after a brush with death. How did I survive such a fall? What did this fall mean? This incident brought up the obvious question of fate and my purpose in life. Climbing had defined my life, it was in my blood, yet when people asked me why I did it, I struggled for words to explain. I couldn't imagine my life without climbing, but where was I headed on that journey? Having nearly lost my life in a moment of absentmindedness, I realized that I needed to pay more attention.

Suddenly everything in my existence had a question mark looming over it. I realized it was time for Lynn to have a close look at Lynn.

Then I reentered the refuge of sleep.

Chapter 2

Early Days

I believe that every event in life happens for a reason. The consequences of my carelessness on the rock that day were like an unexpected slap to the face: stinging but enlightening. In the weeks following the fall at Buoux I came to see my brush with death as an awakening. It was time to pay attention not just to how I climbed, but to how I lived.

That new sense of awareness began the morning after that first day in the hospital in Marseilles. I woke with a clear head. Gone were the gloomy clouds of disappointment that had closed around me when I had seen the extent of my injuries. It was as if during my sleeping hours I had told myself, *I know my body—I'll recover from these injuries.*

There was no one to blame for my accident except myself, and it was my responsibility to drag myself down the road to recovery. That road began in the hospital with a series of X rays and electrical tests that revealed no head injuries and no broken bones other than a hairline fracture in my foot.

My elbow, though, had been wrenched sideways and dislocated when I smashed through the tree. Although the French doctor had popped it back into place, my elbow ligaments, tendons, and cartilage had been painfully torn and stretched. The elbow is one of the most sensitive joints of the body, and to climb again I would have to work hard to restore its strength and flexibility.

But my body was not the only part of me in need of rebuilding. Lying in that stark white ward, I thought about my life of the past few years. My primary focus had been to climb my absolute best, and I had shaped my world around that desire. The result was a whirlwind of travel and rock climbing and physical training. This was precisely the life I wanted, but by letting climbing take precedence, I had let many important things slip to the back of my mind. I found myself thinking about the relationships with family and friends that had helped form the person I had become. I began to realize that my intense focus on climbing had prevented me from confronting imbalances in my personal life. If my life had not flashed before me during my fall, it ran through my thoughts in that French hospital.

My life began in Detroit, Michigan, in 1961. I was the fifth-born in a family of seven blue-eyed children. My father, James Alan Hill, and my mother, Suzanne Biddy, both came from small Catholic families. My father was a descendant of European immigrants who had come to the promised land of America in the late 1800s.

In 1895, my great-grandfather, John Fucentese, moved to Michigan from a small village in southern Italy, changed his last name to Hill, and married a woman of German descent from Baden-Baden named Anna Krauth. Their son Frank worked for Lawyers Title Insurance Company in Detroit and married a Scottish woman, Ruth Gilchrist, whose family owned coal mines in West Virginia near the cliffs of the New River Gorge. Perhaps I inherited my wanderlust from my ninety-four-year-old Scottish grandmother, a woman who describes herself as having "hot feet," and whose home is crammed with souvenirs from her world travels.

It is just as likely that I acquired my adventurous spirit from my maternal grandfather of Irish descent, although I never had the chance to meet him. My mother lost her father when she was only six months old. It was the Great Depression and Ralph Biddy was earning $100 a week—more than many folks made in a month—making films and writing stories for the newsreels that played in cinemas. One fateful day Ralph was flying in a small biplane, filming a new streamline train called the Lincoln Zephyr. When the "barnstormer" pilot edged the plane too close to the train, they were sucked into the vacuum behind the speeding engine and crashed.

I recall little of the suburb of Detroit where my family's roots took hold, although when I returned there during a family trip at the age of eleven, I expected to see a place of urban decay. I began to imagine my parents growing up amid boarded-up buildings and rampant crime, but apparently Detroit wasn't so bad when they were children. It was only after we moved that it deteriorated into a place fraught with riots and unemployment from the faltering car industry. In 1962 we moved from Detroit to Columbus, Ohio, where Dad was working toward a Ph.D. in flight mechanics at Ohio State University.

The Hill family, clockwise from left: Bob, me (with the cat), Michael, Trish, Kathy, Tom, and Jim.
(LYNN HILL COLLECTION)

Both of my parents were twenty years old, married just a year, when they had their first child, in 1956. Then, nearly each year thereafter they produced a new baby, until by 1964 we formed a family of nine. I can only imagine the chaos involved in keeping tabs on so many children. According to family lore, the year we moved from Detroit to Ohio—I was an infant at the time—the family was standing around the loaded station wagon, saying good-bye to friends. When the car took off, there was a shout of, "Hold on, don't forget the baby!" I had nearly been inadvertently left behind in the arms of a neighbor.

A few years later we moved to southern California, where my father got a job working for North American Rockwell as an engineer in the aerospace division. We stayed in Fullerton, in Orange County, through-out the rest of my childhood. Our house sat on a hill, and from the end of the street we could look toward Anaheim and see fireworks light the sky at night above the magic kingdom of Disneyland. When I think of the landscape of our quintessentially American suburb, I think of rows of track houses with double garages, wide streets, shopping malls, and occasional oil derricks, their steel arms and wheels grinding like mechanical monsters, silently pumping oil out of the ground.

We rode bikes everywhere, and a short ride from the house brought us to the neighborhood tar pit, a site full of mystery for local children. This tar pit wasn't far from the La Brea tar pits, the famed archeolog-ical site where prehistoric creatures like dinosaurs and mastodons had sunk into a tarry black muck and had in recent times been exhumed. We would run about on the black semi-liquid surface of the local tar pit, leaving imprints of our feet and sometimes even breaking through the skin into the oily ooze underneath. Whenever that happened, we'd scream and run off, lest we sink in and suffer the same fate as the mastodons. Twenty years later, when my sister Trish and I went back to visit our old neighborhood, we found that the fields where we had spent most of our free time were covered in tract homes, and our tar pit playground was surrounded by a high wire fence and posted with a sign:

DANGER

DO NOT ENTER

TOXIC WASTE SITE

Our tar pit playground, where we had imagined that ancient fossils lurked, was in fact a wasteland of industrial poisons dumped by a local oil company.

But not all the fields were so hazardous. Elsewhere in our suburban wilderness I spent hours building forts and hunting reptiles. My brother Tom and my childhood boyfriend Scott showed me how to catch snakes slumbering under old pieces of wood or cardboard. We'd keep them as pets in a glass aquarium at home, along with all the cats, dogs, chickens, turtles, and hamsters that shared our lively household. Unlike most of the girls I knew, I was drawn to the beautiful form, color, and texture of snakes, which I regarded as friendly creatures. But when it came time for the monthly ritual of placing a mouse in the snake cage, I felt sad watching the savage drama of the snake capturing and swallowing the poor mouse. Despite my compassion for all animals, I realized that this sacrifice was a natural part of the life cycle.

Like most dads, my father worked nine-to-five, five days a week, to support the ever-growing family while Mom took care of the home. My mother had studied dental hygiene in college, but being perpetually pregnant and busy caring for all of us, she had no time to work during those early years in California.

An aeronautical engineer with a gift for problem solving, Dad worked on the control panels of the early space shuttles. At home, he developed a knack for tuning out the noise of his family. I remember one day when I was about five I found him reading the newspaper. Not to be deterred, I bounced around in front of him shouting, "Hey, Dad!" The paper stood between us like a wall and no matter how much I shouted, he remained hidden and silent behind it, ignoring me. Time alone was elusive in our family, and as he read the day's news, he was determined to have five minutes without interruption. As a child it never occurred to me that he needed time to himself, because what I wanted most was his undivided attention. But the sheer size of our family made one-on-one parental attention a scarce commodity. Looking back on this period, I realize now how much I craved my father's attention. When he took to calling me Peanut Ears when I was about six years old, I cherished the nickname for no other reason than because it had come from him.

The Hill family comprised a diverse collection of personalities, yet it was age that determined the family pecking order. Kathy, Jim, and Bob were the "big kids," which meant, from my young perspective, that they got to stay up later at night and enjoy more privileges than us "little kids," who were Trish, me, Tom, and Michael. My sister Kathy was the oldest, and she assumed the role of chief administrator over the rest of us. Even outside the family she had a habit of taking charge. So much so that at the age of six she was reprimanded at school for telling other kids what to do in class. Bossiness aside, she was a helpful and dependable source of information for me on matters of growing up, which she was experiencing ahead of us. You could ask Kathy any question at all and she had a reply. Nothing stumped her. If she didn't know the real answer, she'd make one up.

After Kathy came my brothers Jim and Bob. Both of them inherited the red curly hair and freckles of our mother's Irish genes. Jim was the oldest boy and he took full advantage of his position of male seniority. While playacting a cowboy TV show called *The Roy Rogers and Dale Evans Show* that was popular at the time, Jim, the forceful personality of our troupe, would always assume the star role of Roy. Kathy played the lovely Dale Evans. And Bob, who was youngest in the line of "big kids," was left with the role of Cowboy Nothing. Nevertheless, he always played his role in a good-natured way. Like the rest of us, he learned to adapt to the rules of survival that govern a large family. One of our favorite family sayings was, "If you snooze, you lose." This meant that if there was a half gallon of ice cream in the freezer, you'd better get some before it disappeared. One day Bob thought he'd be clever and stash a Popsicle away in his drawer to eat later. He was disappointed when he discovered the Popsicle had melted all over his clothes.

My sister Trish was the leader of us "little kids." Though she was the middle child, she aspired to be one of the big kids. I was so far down the line that I had no other choice but to accept my rank as a little kid. Trish and I shared the same room throughout childhood. Much to my mother's annoyance we would chatter endlessly after lights-out time, which brought her to the door several times a night with a stern whisper to "Be quiet! Go to sleep!" To foil Mom, we devised a phone system made from two paper cups linked by a string; into these kid-phones we talked, bed to bed. Maybe it was because we had complementary personalities that the pair of us got along like best friends. While Kathy and I tended to be serious and pragmatic by nature, Trish had a more flirtatious approach to life. Cute, girlish charm was Trish's strong suit, and she knew how to use it on babysitters, teachers, or any boy she wanted to win over. In school, Trish seemed to have just the right blend of charisma and intelligence to excel. Though I did fine in school, I felt most in my element while playing outside.

My birth followed Trish's by fifteen months. One of the classic family stories about us relates to when I was about two years old. My Aunt Gale mentioned that I didn't speak much. Trish, who was three at the time, replied by saying, "She talks but nobody listens." Being heard in such a large family was never easy, so instead I learned to engage in my own world and to figure things out on my own. I can still hear my mother's words from those years: "If you want something done, do it yourself." I embraced her philosophy early and this approach has stayed with me ever since. Apparently, by age three I insisted on tying my own shoes. Whether by nature or by necessity, or a bit of both, I learned to be independent and self-sufficient.

As far as a presage to my career as a climber, there is a quote from my baby journal that reads, "Lynn climbs the monkey bars like a pro." Climbing movement seemed natural and alluring to me from the earliest days. By age twelve I had invented a method of climbing up the neighborhood light pole using a technique similar to that of a coconut tree climber. I wrapped my hands around the cement pole while clamping my bare feet against opposing sides and climbed up it for 25 feet. My technique for getting down involved sliding down the rough-textured pole like a fireman. The other kids in the neighborhood were impressed, but my mother looked on with bemused concern. Little did she know where this would lead.

Next in line after me came my brothers Tom and Michael. Tom was the hyperactive child of the family. When he was two, my mother had to lock the deadbolt on our front door because Tom had developed a nocturnal urge to explore the neighborhood. Like a pint-sized escape artist, he would wait until everyone was asleep, climb out of his crib, unlatch the door, and wander the surrounding streets and yards in the dead of night. Once my mother found Tom inside a chicken coop in our neighbor's front yard at six A.M., the hens huddled nervously at one end, and our naked and chicken-shit-covered Tom at the other. My mother used to call him Tom Terrific after a cartoon show about a young superboy and his wonder dog, both of whom found trouble everywhere.

At school, Tom had a hard time sitting still in class and was often sent to the principal's office for causing trouble. He even bit the principal once when he was being reprimanded. Whenever possible, I stuck up for "Yom," as I used to affectionately call him (he called me "Yinn"). One day when I was about eight years old, I saw that a particularly heavyweight neighborhood bully was picking on Tom, and I wasn't sure what to do. Later that night, I rehearsed the way I would defend him in the future. I sat on the counter in front of the bathroom mirror and pursed my lips and clenched my teeth, imitating Robert Redford's tough-guy look in *Butch Cassidy and the Sundance Kid*. I practiced my line: "Leave my little brother alone or I'll beat you up." Just as I finished saying this, I noticed my mother watching my performance in the hallway and we both burst out laughing.

Michael was the adorable baby of the family. As a toddler, if he didn't get his way, he would bang his head against the car window. For several months he had a large bump on his forehead. At that time I couldn't imagine what Michael would be like as a mature individual. But then again, as a young girl I couldn't imagine what it would be like to have a separate life outside my close-knit family. I'll never forget when this thought first occurred to me. We were on a family camping trip, traveling by night in our camping trailer. I was about nine years old and Jim was thirteen and we had crawled into a nest of sleeping bags and pillows in the overhead bunk, where Jim began reciting a song he'd made up about our family. Each of us was the subject of a mocking verse, which my talented brother punctuated with musical fart noises. I laughed until my stomach hurt. Then he suddenly stopped singing.

"You know, one day when we're all grown up, we'll have families of our own and we won't live together anymore," he said after a studied pause.

It saddened me to think that he was right, that someday the family would be scattered across the country and would no longer share our day-to-day lives. But for the moment our family seemed indestructibly happy, every bit the *Brady Bunch* model that American families seemed to aspire to. Our family was even selected to pose for a Kodak advertisement, and as the photographer had us all parade in front of our sub-

My parents, Sue and Jim, on one of our family trips to the beach. (LYNN HILL COLLEC-
TION)

urban home with our tricycles and toys, we were one big happy family
in glowing color. Little did I know then that there's no such thing as a
perfect family.

Those family camping trips were some of the best times of my childhood. When I was a toddler, we spent nearly every weekend waterski-
ing at nearby Lake Elsinore. Then came our sailing phase. First, Dad
bought a little sabot, then he worked up to a Hobie 14. Later he got
together with some friends and bought a twenty-four-foot sailboat.
When we attempted to sail the twenty-six miles from Newport Harbor
to Catalina Island on this small yacht, nearly everyone became seasick
except Dad and me; Mom was smart enough to stay home. So ill were
my siblings that halfway to Catalina we turned about and headed
home. That was our first and last major family sailing trip. After that
we reverted back to long trips by station wagon to the mountains,
deserts, or lakes, where we enjoyed the big-sky views of the western
states.

The year I turned thirteen, one of our drives took us north from LA,
past Bakersfield, and up the Merced River. As we rounded the last bend

coming out of the Wawona tunnel, the full view of Yosemite Valley stunned me like no other landscape before. Goose bumps raced across my body as I stared at the marbled walls of El Capitan. To its right I saw more cliffs and a waterfall cascading in a great arc, sending slow-moving waves of mist into the air. Half Dome, a huge semicircle of rock, crowned the end of the valley. I knew people climbed these cliffs—Kathy's new boyfriend, Chuck, had just graduated from a rock climbing course and had told me about Yosemite—but I couldn't imagine how anyone could climb a wall as sheer and as high as El Capitan.

When they weren't taking us on trips along America's scenic roads, my parents wisely immersed us in activities that harnessed our abundant physical energy. Since Dad dabbled in Californian pursuits like surfing and cross-country skiing, so did we. Skateboarding, roller-skating, softball, baseball, football, and summer camp were all activities we enjoyed. My mother juggled our complex sports schedules and shuttled everyone around from one activity to the next in our station wagon.

Dad busied himself with the boys' activities, coaching Jim and Bob's football and baseball teams and chaperoning Michael's Indian Guides group, an organization similar to Boy Scouts. One of the activities that Mom participated in with us girls was Bluebirds, the female version of Indian Guides. But instead of learning to make fire by rubbing two sticks together, as the boys did, we made wall hangings and other "feminine" homemaker-style crafts. I envied the fire makers and their camping trip to Joshua Tree and wondered why girls couldn't do it too.

It took me years to fully appreciate the meaning of my mother's words when she said that I "marched to the beat of a different drummer." But looking back now, I realize that I was never the type of girl who liked dressing up in uncomfortable clothes and wearing makeup. I felt better wearing blue jeans, climbing trees, and catching snakes and lizards in the fields near our neighborhood. Such unfeminine endeavors earned me the label "tomboy." Despite the negative stigma then attached to the term, this never deterred me from pursuing my own natural inclinations.

Everyone in the Hill family pursued their own interests outside the family, but the one activity that we all had in common was swimming. When my mother started part-time work as a dental hygienist, she would drop us all off at the Los Coyotes Country Club, where we trained and competed on the swim team. One experience stands out in my memory from those early days, and it concerns the last important race of the year. I was just seven years old, but already I had been promoted to the more advanced "all-star" level swim team. The night before the event, there was a party with music and dancing at the country club. My coach, whom I adored, picked me up and danced with me in his arms. When he asked me to do my best in this race, I felt a powerful motivation to win. For him. I was deep in puppy love with this man.

The morning of the race, while standing on the starting blocks waiting for the sound of the starting gun, I felt a ball of energy in my stomach. At the sound of the starting gun I exploded into a dive and hit the water. The race was a fifty-yard freestyle sprint, and on the final stretch I noticed a competitor in the neighboring lane closing in on my lead. Threatened with losing, I concentrated all my force to make one final stroke to the finish line. Barely grazing the tips of my fingers on the wall at the end of the pool, I emerged smiling, convinced I had won.

But the judges hadn't seen my fingertip finish and minutes after the race my coach broke the news to me that I had been disqualified. I felt a hollow sense of disappointment with myself. Though just a child, I realized that if I hadn't been so concerned about "winning," I might have followed my own natural rhythm and won anyway. This was a lesson that became imprinted on my memory: don't let the desire to win interfere with your performance.

Although swimming was an ideal activity for building a basic athletic foundation as a child, the training process of endlessly lapping a pool was unbearably monotonous. Fortunately, I soon found another interest to replace swimming. One day, going with my mother to pick up my brother at the YMCA, I caught sight of a full-fledged gymnasium for the first time. Fascinated by the sleek, honed bodies whirling around on the bars and rings and flipping around on the exercise mats, I suddenly found myself joining in by performing a few cartwheels. One of the guys watched me cartwheel past.

"Pretty good. Can you do a round-off?" he said.

"What's that?"

"I'll show you."

He demonstrated the move. A round-off is an advanced variation of the cartwheel, but instead of letting your legs circle around your body like the spokes of a wheel, they are brought together in midair so you can land on them solidly together, facing the direction you came from. After the gymnast demonstrated the move, he offered to show me other techniques. Learning how to perform acrobatic moves in a gym seemed more fun than anything I'd done before. While I learned tricks from the gymnast, my mother waited patiently outside in the car. This would mark the first of many trips to this place and the awakening of my life-time passion of playing with the forces of gravity.

The YMCA gymnastics program was in an early stage of development when I joined. I was one of only two girls in the group. But over the next few years our growing team performed in exhibitions at local schools, did halftime shows at the Angels Baseball Stadium, and competed in gymnastics competitions all over southern California. Our afternoon practice sessions allowed me to explore the capacity of my body, as well as my mind and imagination. For the first time I understood that phys-ical action isn't only physical, but has a mental component as well.

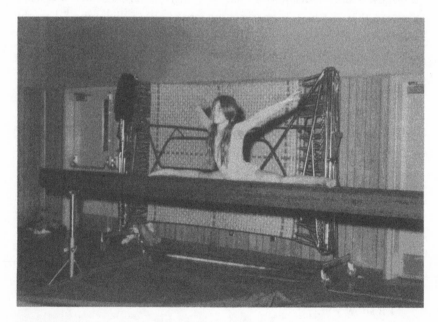

On the balance beam at the local YMCA. (LYNN HILL COLLECTION)

This essential element of performance dawned on me one day during practice when I had just broken through the mental barrier of being able to perform a round-off, backhand spring, and back flip all in sequence, without help from a "spotter"—someone to catch me if I made a mistake. As I waited for a ride home after practice, I sat alone in the gym thinking how confident I had felt performing this tumbling maneuver by myself. On an impulse I stood up and launched into the series of flips again.

Just as my legs began to circle around overhead, the thought flashed through my mind that perhaps this was a bad idea. If I hurt myself, no one would be there to help me. Suddenly I froze in midair. The next thing I knew, I was lying on my upper back and neck on the mat. I wasn't hurt, but this experience taught me not to let fear interrupt my concentration once I was committed to action. That element of gym philosophy would, in time, translate into an important part of climbing philosophy for me.

My coach, Scott Crouse, was a former competitive gymnast on the California State University at Fullerton gymnastics team, and week by week he taught me more complex maneuvers. One day he suggested that I try a double back flip. I had seen a few world-class gymnasts like Kathy Rigby execute such difficult moves, and while I had a mental image of what a double back flip looked like, I wasn't sure how to translate this visual information into action.

"Just concentrate on three simple steps: the initial jump, tucking into a ball, and the final landing on the ground," Scott explained.

The thought of attempting this very advanced movement was daunting, but I trusted Scott to spot me well. As I practiced the double back flip, I mentally replayed what the flip looked and felt like each time I performed it. I discovered that I could dismantle the movement and focus on each separate phase of it, as if it were a series of photographs. This method of learning, called "chunking," was an effective means of understanding the components of movement in simple steps. At the age of eleven, I had discovered a powerful learning tool for getting my body to follow whatever my mind imagined. Visual learning, I would later find, also had direct applications to rock climbing.

Scott also emphasized the importance of using proper technique and form in gymnastics. He urged me to pay attention to the precise execution of each movement and to practice as though I were performing in a competition. One of Scott's dictums that still resonates in my memory was, "Once a bad habit is reinforced through repetition, it's hard to change. The brain tends to imprint incorrect movement patterns just as well as it does correct ones."

"Keep your legs straight and your toes pointed," he'd remind me.

One day while watching a performance by Shelly Lewins, one of the best gymnasts in the region, I suddenly understood the interrelationship between form and function. Shelly moved her arms and legs in perfectly linear or circular paths of movement. When she performed a split-leap, she was able to achieve maximum amplitude and perfect symmetry in the air by thrusting her arms and legs at precisely the right moment. In making transitions from one position to another, her arms flowed in graceful curves, or, conversely, in explosive thrusts to create efficient movement and aesthetic beauty all at once. This kind of perfection in movement was inspiring and clearly an effort worth working toward.

But as an eager young girl, I was more interested in learning complex acrobatic maneuvers than focusing on pretty formalities. The cute poses, stylish hand gestures, and fake smiles I was expected to display while performing competitions went against my nature. They seemed contrived and artificial and I resisted them. I did my routines with strength and agility and I did them deadpan and with few flourishes. Judges were not entirely impressed. As gymnastics became more rigid and structured, I began to lose my motivation and enthusiasm for remaining on the team.

At that time, entering adolescence, I felt resistant to rules. My nonconformist attitude was probably a reflection of normal teenage uppityness, but perhaps I was also influenced by the socially turbulent environment around me. The Vietnam War had ended a few years before and kids of my era had been exposed to some of the rebelliousness of that time. My awareness of issues like women's rights and the struggle for racial freedom began to grow. In 1973, at the age of twelve, I decided I'd had enough of competitive gymnastics and I quit the YMCA team.

As a teenager, I began to question authority and the traditional roleplaying that occurred within my own family. Around the house the division of chores between the boys and girls seemed unfair. The boys only had a few tasks they had to do, like take out the garbage and mow the lawn, each a weekly event. But washing dishes and cleaning the house—an endless drudgery—fell to the girls. When I heard the phrase "a woman's work is never done," I understood why. Looking at the newspaper or TV, I wondered why women did most of the practical work while men controlled most of the power and money. It took me years to understand how women have developed other sources of empowerment to balance out the inequalities in external power.

By the time I entered the optimistically named Sunny Hills High School at the age of fourteen, I was aware that not all the world resembled southern California. Our suburb of Hollywood was the epitome of wholesome, white-bread America. It seemed to me that everyone around me was following some version of the latest trend they had seen on TV, like caricatures of the movie sets a few miles away. As for my own fashion sense—so key to fitting into the teen social scene—Trish summed me up succinctly: "You were clueless." Moreover, I didn't care. I had just discovered the world of rock climbing and this was the environment and community that I could identify with.

My life took a fateful turn that summer of 1975 when I jumped into the back of my oldest sister's fiancée's truck and traveled to a small climbing area in southern California called Big Rock. In the front seat sat Kathy with her long-haired boyfriend, Chuck Bludworth. In the back were me, my sister Trish, and my brother Bob, who was Chuck's climbing partner. Neither Trish nor I had ever climbed, and I was still uncertain how climbers even "got the rope up there"—an innocent question, I would later learn, that is often posed by tourists. The back of Chuck's blue Ford pickup—a present for his sixteenth birthday from his adoring parents—was strewn with strange-looking climbing gadgets, such as hexagonal metal objects threaded with loops of brightly colored nylon rope. I had no idea how these objects could be used to climb a cliff. As our truck ambled through the endless sprawl of shopping malls, suburbs, and cement freeways of LA, and I flicked through Chuck's well-thumbed copy of *Basic Rock Craft,* by Royal Robbins, I became no wiser to this odd-looking sport. I saw pages full of confusing diagrams of burly, unshaven men executing rope stunts and tying complicated knots, and the text was filled with new words like "piton," "prusik," and "carabiner." But Chuck had frequently reminded me that "you'd be good at it since you're light and strong from gymnastics."

After driving an hour and a half from our home in Orange County to just outside Riverside and hiking thirty minutes over an arid hillside, we arrived at the base of a 300-foot-high white granite slab called Big Rock, inclined at the angle of a steep ski run. The hot air carried the sweet odor of sage and a fresh smell from nearby Lake Parris. We dumped our rucksacks at the foot of the cliff, and I watched Chuck methodically sort through his jangling array of gear. Lizards darted up the rock wall, skating lightly up the smooth face on their tiny claws. But to me, the face appeared to be devoid of holds.

"Why don't you girls start on this easy climb while Bob and I do another climb nearby?" Chuck suggested.

Kathy pointed to the route that Chuck had suggested we try. The Trough was its inauspicious name, and she set about gearing Trish up for action.

Kathy (right) in her usual position of command at the base of the cliff, with Gary Cox belaying. (LYNN HILL COLLECTION)

"Okay," Kathy said, "first comes the swami belt harness."

This was the era of climbing before comfortable and adjustable harnesses with leg loops and buckled waist belts became popular among climbers. She wrapped a long strand of one-inch-wide nylon webbing around Trish's waist and then rigged a loop around her legs. She knotted the ends together and tied the climbing rope into the whole affair.

"This stuff looks like nothing but an old seat belt salvaged off a car," I said distrustfully as she finished Trish's knot.

"Well, yeah, but if it's strong enough for a car, it's certainly strong enough to hold you," was Kathy's confident reply.

Then she demonstrated how to execute the dreaded "body belay." This was also before the advent of mechanical belay devices that automatically create friction on the rope to prevent it from slipping in the case of a fall.

"This is your brake hand," she said while gripping the rope in her right hand. "If the climber falls, you stop them like this," at which point she wrapped the rope tight around her buttock and hip.

It looked painful, bound to produce rope burn. I crinkled my nose at the thought of having to hold a fall.

"Never let go of the rope with your brake hand," Kathy added with a solemn tone.

"Why?" I asked.

"Because if you do, the climber will hit the deck. Now it's time for someone to lead the climb." Kathy spoke directly to Trish.

Trish and I rarely questioned Kathy's leadership, but I thought it odd that Kathy would hand the responsibility of leading over to her novice sister. Trish and I didn't know that even though Kathy was well grounded in the basics of climbing, she was terrified of the exposed feeling that leading up a route produces.

Trish shuffled toward the cliff, looking uncertain. She wore climbing shoes called RDs. The name was derived from the initials of the famous French mountaineer René Desmaison, who had designed them. On Trish they were oversized and oafish gumboots and the hard black rubber soles clunked like wooden clogs when she placed them against the rock. I started laughing at Trish's ungainly appearance.

"Shut up," she yelled, laughing back at me.

"Where do I go?" Trish then asked in a nervous tone.

"You see those metal bolts sticking out of the rock? Follow those and clip these carabiners into them. Then clip your rope through the carabiner," Kathy answered.

Our route was an easy 5.4 grade, yet for a beginner the first climb is always a mystery and an ordeal. Trish headed upward toward the first bolt, clipped it as instructed, then kept moving to the second bolt. I could hear her labored breathing growing louder. Her feet slipped about and her hands fondled the rock with uncertainty.

Thirty feet off the ground and with two bolts clipped, Trish then got lost by veering left from the natural line of handholds onto a sheet of rock that to her looked easier. But when she saw the consequences of her detour—she was now far away from the protection bolts and facing a big fall if she slipped—her voice grew higher in pitch.

"What do I do now?"

"You need to climb back to the right and clip into another bolt," Kathy replied.

"What would happen if she fell?" I posed this hypothetical question to Kathy while Trish fumbled, shook, and whimpered.

Kathy calmly explained the mechanism of the protection system: If Trish were to fall, she would fall the length of rope between where she stood and the last bolt she had clipped, plus that far again as she fell past the bolt. The rope, which is clipped through the carabiner and bolt, would then catch her, but there would also be a few added feet of fall due to the stretch in the rope and the inevitable slide through Kathy's hands. I thought about this and it appeared that Trish, who was now thirty-five feet above the ground, was so high above her last protection bolt that she would hit the ground before the rope would catch her. *This looks dangerous,* I thought.

Then Trish's legs started trembling violently.

"Why are her legs shaking like that?" I asked.

"Sewing machine leg," Kathy answered cryptically. Because Trish was poised on the edges of her feet and had all her weight bearing down on them, the nervous tension in the muscles was causing her legs to gyrate up and down, like the needle of a sewing machine.

Trish inched back over to the protection bolt. When she clipped the rope through the carabiner, she grabbed it with both hands and hung, panting.

"Can I come down now?"

Kathy lowered her. I didn't bother to ask Trish how she liked the climb. It was evident from watching her trembling hands untie the rope that she didn't enjoy it. In fact, it would be eighteen years before she tried the sport again with her two young sons, in the shelter of an indoor climbing facility in Salt Lake City.

"Okay, Lynn, your turn now," said Kathy with her usual authority. But rather than try the Trough again, Kathy decided I would lead another route nearby that turned out to be even harder.

Trish handed me the RD climbing shoes. A full size too big, they felt clumsy on my feet. Kathy helped me tie into the rope, handed me a bunch of carabiners, and sent me on my way. After climbing several moves, I looked over my shoulder to the ground. I understood right away why Trish had looked so alarmed. I looked back up and saw the bolt, a rusty outpost of alleged safety, still several feet above me. *What have I gotten myself into?* I thought. Unlike gymnastics, there was no spotter to keep me from falling to the ground. And instead of facing gym mats, I was looking down at a hard rocky landing.

"Try to friction your feet against the face," Kathy suggested.

I set my feet against the rock, latched my fingertips firmly around a couple of small flakes, then began moving upward. My feet held, as if glued to the cliff. As clutzy as those RDs looked, their smooth rubber soles were doing their job.

I felt a sense of relief when I arrived at the first bolt and clipped my rope into it. But as soon as I made a few moves past it, I felt a sting of adrenaline in my gut when I thought about the consequences of a fall. With each step upward, I felt more vulnerable as I moved farther away from the security of my protection bolt. But rather than looking down toward the ground, I decided to maintain my focus on the rock ahead.

"Just keep going," I said to myself as I continued up the wall, clipping into one bolt after another. This process of hanging and standing on small edges and bumps on the rock seemed much more delicate and insecure than I had imagined climbing would be. The farther I went, the more my muscles ached. When I arrived at what my sister called the anchor—the point at which I had completed the climb and could lower back down to the ground—I felt an immediate sense of relief and sat-isfaction.

When I arrived back on the ground, a woman with a beaming smile said to me, "Good job! Was that your first climb?"

Unbeknownst to me, the person speaking was Maria Cranor, one of the few women climbing at a high level back then and someone with whom I would form a lasting friendship. From the first day I met her, she was a source of inspiration and encouragement to me, as she was to all her friends and colleagues.

By the end of the day I knew I had been hooked on some new sen-sation. As we walked down the hill back to the car, I watched the late afternoon sun turn the granite orange and highlight every nubbin and detail on its surface. Already I began to associate the beautiful form and texture of the rock with my desire to climb it. From that day on, I never saw a cliff in exactly the same way again.

Chapter 3

First
Contact

"Hey, Lynnie, you want the sharp end?" yelled Chuck from up on the cliff 25 feet above me, where he dangled at the end of the climbing rope. He had just fallen from the hardest section of a climb called Trespassers Will Be Violated at a climbing area in the Mojave Desert known as Joshua Tree.

"The what?" I answered, not knowing what the sharp end was.

Chuck laughed his braying, horsey laugh. "The sharp end is my end—the leader's end. I'm asking you if you want to lower me down to where you are and then you can come up here and try to lead this route. I can't see a way to climb past this section."

Only a few weeks had passed since Chuck and Kathy had introduced me to the world of climbing at Big Rock. I had led a few more routes since then. When I tagged along with Chuck and Bob, I followed behind

Chuck Bludworth (center), my brother Bob, and me gearing up for a day of climbing. (CHARLIE ROW)

on the safer "blunt end" of the rope, with Chuck secured to the rock, ready to catch me on the rope if I slipped. Even so, it had become apparent that I had a talent for drifting fairly easily up the climbs we did—sometimes more easily than Chuck, Bob, or Kathy.

I leaned my head out and looked up at the section of the climb where Chuck had slid off. Twice he had climbed out sideways from the first protection bolt, and twice he had become infected with sewing machine leg. One lesson I'd learned was that once sewing machine leg sets in, it is only a matter of seconds before the climber falls off. Sure enough, Chuck had come careening off the "crux"—the climb's hardest section—precisely on sewing machine leg schedule, and he had swung sideways for twenty feet by the time the rope, running through the carabiner and the piece of protection it was clipped to, arrested his fall. Belaying him at the other end of that rope, I was jerked up against the cliff by the impact. Chuck easily outweighed me by forty-five pounds, and I was feeling like a passenger in a car that had been repeatedly rear-ended.

"Sure, I'll try it."

At this point in my climbing career I knew little about the rating system that climbers use to differentiate between one climb that is easy and another that is harder. The rating scale as we know it today in the American system contains about twenty-five degrees of difficulty, from 5.0 at the beginning level to 5.15 at the top end. Like the belt system in martial arts, each number and letter grade indicates the relative degree of difficulty. In 1976, when I was tying into the sharp end of the rope to try Trespassers Will Be Violated, the top end of the rating scale was 5.11. The climb Chuck had talked me into leading was rated 5.10+ and it was also poorly protected, since there were only three bolts on the entire 80-foot climb. Diving into a climb as hard as that with my fledgling experience was a little like dropping into an expert "black diamond" chute when you'd just gotten past mastering the snowplow in skiing. In other words, it was potentially reckless. But I had no idea what I was getting into.

After I lowered Chuck down to the ground, we traded ends and I headed back up over the vertical terrain he had already covered. Around me sprawled Joshua Tree's surreal landscape. Thousands of blobs of rock between 50 and 200 feet tall dotted the desert floor for miles in every direction. Depending on your bent of imagination, it either resembled the aftermath of a meteor shower or a parade of giant desert tortoises, as each granite dome was distinctly carapace-shaped. Chuck, being a geology major, was always lecturing our climbing clan about the rocks we grappled with, and he identified the rock here as a type of granite called quartz monzonite. To me, it seemed like a coarse, granular type of rock, and as I traversed sideways to the point where Chuck had plummeted, I saw the reason he had fallen: this patch of granite had virtually no holds on it.

All I had to work with was a slabby surface of rock textured with crystals the size of grape seeds. Only if I could perch my toes and wrap my fingertips around these tiny, sharp clusters would the traverse in front of me be feasible. To move forward required a combination of brutish finger strength, balletlike toe pointing, and fluid balance. If I faltered along the traverse and stopped out of concern that I was getting too far away from my protection, then I'd slide off like Chuck. Although my range of climbing experience was minimal, I found I could look at the rock in front of me and analyze the situation as if it were an abstract problem: the rock features and my body were elements of the puzzle and the correct answer lay in me reaching the other end of the traverse. If I connected the moves accurately, getting my body in the most efficient position to continue moving fluidly, then I would solve the problem. Any single wrong move and I would lose my strength and fall.

"Okay, Chuck, here goes," I said as I set off.

As I moved sideways like a crab scuttling along the shoreline, I realized I had never climbed anything as demanding as this before. The combination of controlling every position of my body and of forcing my mind to shut out the ever-present urge to submit to the very real fear of falling created an interesting result: a feeling that I was simultaneously acutely aware of both everything and nothing. Everything, because twenty-five years later I still recall the kaleidoscope of crystal patterns in the rock in front of me as I moved over it, and nothing, because at the time I was so immersed in the passage of movement that I felt no sense of time, gravity or existence. The only sound I heard was the flow of my breathing.

I continued past the point where Chuck had fallen, moved several more feet across the grainy rock slab, and found myself eyeing a protection bolt an arm's reach away. All I had to do was clip the bolt with a carabiner and clip the rope into that and I would be home free. But my body was splayed across the rock like a starfish, and I felt that releasing one hand from the rock to grab a carabiner from the bandolier slung around my neck would cause me to peel off of the face.

"Keep it together Lynnie. You can do it," Chuck's voice rose up, barely registering with my thoughts.

But my momentum had stalled. Fear had set in. Sewing machine leg was building up in the ball of my foot. My forearms were bloating and aching as blood swelled the veins. I had to think fast. The options presented themselves. I could reach out quickly and wrap two of my fingers through the steel eye of the bolt and hang from one finger. But no, that would be as digit-friendly as grabbing a knife. Anyway, the rules of the game dictated that the bolt was there only to protect me, not to support my weight; if I grabbed it, I'd be guilty of bad free-climbing style. Option two then became clear: I had to calm my nerves and keep going past the bolt to a more secure place to stand. From there I could more easily clip the bolt.

I took a couple of deep breaths and climbed on. My gambit worked, and a second later I was clipping a carabiner to the bolt, feeling a tingle of new energy running through my body. Minutes later I reached the top of the dome and I was rigging an anchor, then pulling in rope and belaying Chuck up to me.

"Awesome, Lynn, awesome," he gasped when he reached me.

That night around the campfires at Joshua Tree the local expert climbers were sipping beers, talking about "the girl who'd led Trespassers." I didn't know it at the time, but the climb had a serious reputation and had scared several experienced climbers out of their wits.

If I could choose one person to call my first mentor of climbing, it would be my partner that day on Trespassers Will Be Violated. Chuck Bludworth opened my eyes to the world of climbing and taught me something about its heart and soul. Chuck encouraged me to get on the rock and do my best. He never fell prey to the insecurity of being outdone by a young, novice girl.

Chuck and my sister Kathy had been childhood sweethearts since their teens. They'd gone to the high school prom together, they began climbing together, and they would marry in 1977, when they were twenty-two and twenty-one, respectively. A photo of them together taken the night of the prom shows them dressed in formal attire, my sister with a corsage, and a bearded Chuck with a mane of blond, wavy locks that almost matched the length of Kathy's Rapunzel-like hair.

Chuck had initiated the climbing experiment for Kathy and my brother Bob, but while they merely saw it as an interesting weekend diversion, Chuck looked at climbing as a way of life. He regarded climbing as a thing of beauty and mystery. A sunset of red clouds against which the otherworldly forms of shaggy-leafed Joshua trees and rock domes were silhouetted in the twilight, viewed from the top of our last climb of the day, represented to Chuck a deep connection between himself and the land. He saw climbing as a kind of spiritual journey, not unlike the vision quests that Native Americans put themselves through. The ritual of preparing and planning for a climb, of embarking on the journey, of testing yourself with fear and exhaustion in a risky setting, all spoke to some part of Chuck's deeper self.

This was the period of the 1970s when the Brave New World of mind expansion through any means was hip, and the novels of Carlos Castaneda were in vogue. Those books were part of nearly every climber's book collection. A *Separate Reality* and *Tales of Power* described a mystical journey through Yaqui Indian sorcery, replete with encounters with spirits that were accessed by mind-controlling rituals with drugs like peyote. Climbing was a sacred vehicle that could lift these J-Tree aficionados out of the daily grind of life in the concrete jungle of LA and take them to another plane.

With his Merlin-like hair and his bent for the mystical, Chuck cut a striking swath through my teens. One day as I was strolling down a street with Chuck, we passed an unoccupied parked car and the radio suddenly turned itself on. Chuck immediately insinuated that this had happened because of his powerful magnetic presence. In some ways he was pulling my leg, yet in other ways there was a side to Chuck that believed exactly that.

Even more than rock climbing, Chuck idealized mountaineering in the high ranges as the epitome of the spiritual quest. Chuck's bookshelves were lined with volumes penned by famous alpinists of the day like Reinhold Messner and Walter Bonatti. Messner wrote with Germanic seriousness about climbing in the "death zone," a frigid realm some-where above 26,000 feet. In one book Messner described his ordeals on the Himalayan peak Nanga Parbat, one of the fourteen peaks above 8000 meters (26,000 feet), on which he and his brother Günther had climbed a hard new route. On the climb back down the other side of the mountain an avalanche killed Günther, and Reinhold, alone and lost, suffered days of starvation and anguish. By the time native shepherds found him he was a mere rail of a man, with such severe frostbite that his toes had to be amputated. Astonishingly, a couple of years later Messner returned to the same face on which his brother had been crushed under tons of ice and climbed Nanga Parbat again—alone. On this ascent Messner wrote of ghosts, spirits, hallucinations, and of feeling a sense of closeness to the realm of death that the combination of high altitude, physical depriva-tion, and his own near-death experience had created.

Chuck aspired to such extremes of adventure. I, on the other hand, listened to such tales and never quite understood his attraction to the frozen realm. From a young age I saw the mountains as being cold, rugged, and unstable places. Though I could appreciate a kind of austere beauty in such high places, it was nothing like the type of climbing with which I had begun to bond. I felt a strong sense of belonging in Joshua Tree's sun-soaked landscape, with its tawny-red stone dappled with cactus-green. In this desert playground I felt a sense of harmony among the forms and shapes of nature.

Nevertheless, all climbing was exciting to me and Chuck easily persuaded me to visit the "mini-mountains" of the Sierra Nevada range. Temple Crag is a semi-alpine-style peak in the Palisades Range of the Sierras, and in the summer of 1976, when I was fifteen years old, we carried our backpacks over alpine meadows, shivered through the night

Chuck climbing in the Sierra Nevadas. (BOB HILL)

in our inadequate sleeping bags in a small tent, and then at first light set out up a scree slope toward the west face.

I had never climbed snow or ice. When we were confronted by a barrier of firm snow on a slope of about forty-five degrees, we had to kick steps into it to prevent our feet from sliding off. Of course, on a real alpine expedition the climbers would be wearing crampons over their stiff-soled, waterproof mountain boots, and they'd be swinging an ice ax into the snow slope. But Chuck and I wore sneakers for the approach to the climb, and the closest thing to an ice tool we had was a hammer, designed for driving in pitons, that sported a short, pointy pick on the other end of the hammerhead. It looked more like a gardening tool than an ice ax, and as it belonged to Chuck, he led the way, using it to cut steps in the hard snow.

When we stepped off the snowfield at the base of the summit tower, we tied the rope onto our harnesses and began climbing up a cliff comprised of shattered alpine granite. First I slotted my hips into a wide fissure and shimmied up; then, higher, we encountered pitches on which cube-shaped blocks the size of TV sets poised on ledges, looking ready to tumble off with the slightest brush of an elbow. While we climbed, pitch after pitch, slotting in nuts, Chuck, the geology expert, explained why the rock resembled a badly stacked china cabinet.

"It's because of the action of freeze and thaw," he explained. "During the day the snow slopes on top of the cliff melt and water trickles into the gaps between blocks. When the water freezes in the cold of night, the ice expands, acting like a crowbar that forces the rocks to fracture and break apart. The process takes eons, but it ensures that most mountain climbs are comprised of tottering rubble."

"Are the Himalayas and Andes loose like this?" I asked, having recently heard him talk in awe of those ranges.

"If anything, they are way worse," he replied. "The taller the peak, the more shattered the rock."

"That does it, I'm never going there. I'll stick to dry solid rock in the sun," I replied.

We didn't get to the summit of Temple Crag. A long ridge lay between us and the pointed top, and it looked like a dump truck had emptied a quarry-load of boulders all over it. There was no way I was going to paw my way over such life-threatening rubble just for the sake of getting to the top. We had climbed the route—ten pitches of 5.9—and that was good enough for me.

Thumbing through Chuck's library of alpine literature, I had absorbed one thing: that most mountaineering accidents occur on the descent. As we padded down the other side of Temple Crag, the terrain grew steeper and remained covered with delicately perched boulders. At a cliff we had to break out the rope and rappel for 200 feet. If done correctly, rappelling is a safe and easy method of getting down a cliff by hooking a rope through a metal device that is clipped to the harness, and which creates friction so one can slowly slide down the rope. But here, as the sun-cooked Sierra snows melted, small stones were being freed from the snow and were rolling off the slopes, whizzing by us like bullets.

"This is like a shooting gallery," I told Chuck with a sense of alarm.

He smiled as if he'd seen it all before and beckoned me down the rope. At the bottom of the cliff he stood on a narrow bridge of snow that spanned a gaping chasm. As I lowered myself to him, he reached out and grabbed my hand.

"Whatever you do, don't fall into the *bergschrund*," he instructed.

"The what?"

"*Bergschrund*. It's a German word. *Berg* means mountain, *schrund* refers to the gap. It's this void where the snow slope has melted away from the cliff."

"Why don't you just say 'snow gap'?"

"Because mountaineering started in Europe."

We pulled the rope back down from where it had been anchored for our rappel, then prepared to descend the last few hundred feet to the ground. At that point, our only choice of descent was either to climb down the steep exposed snow slope or chimney down between the rock and ice that formed the *bergschrund*. Chuck decided to climb down the snow slope using our only tool while I belayed him from above with no belay anchor. To secure myself from being pulled off in case Chuck should fall, I sat behind a hump of ice with my feet braced against this natural barrier.

Once Chuck arrived safely down to the ground, he shouted up, "Okay, Lynnie, come down."

Since Chuck had gone down first with our only hammer, I was left with no other choice but to climb down between a slippery wall of ice and the wet rock face, while straddling a three-foot-wide gap. Below me I saw darkness that led into the bowels of the mountain.

My hands and feet went numb as I carefully straddled the dark abyss, placing my bare hands and the smooth soles of my rubber climbing shoes against ice on one side and wet rock on the other. My mind kept flashing on horrifying images of falling into the cold, dark oblivion.

When I got down to where Chuck waited, he held up a hand.

"Watch your step. I fell into a hole just in front of you. I was lucky enough to have stopped on a snow bridge a few feet down, but if I hadn't stopped there, I would have gone down another sixty feet or so."

I felt more at ease when we stepped off the slippery snow onto the thick peaty soil of the meadow. On the hike back down the trail that led through the twisted claws of a pine forest, I marveled at a beautiful crystal I had found while descending the scree field from the top. I wondered how there could be such perfect natural order and beauty in the midst of the random chaos of this mountain environment. The crystal seemed to be a symbolic reminder of the duality of nature. True, the high dry Sierra air and the views of rolling thunderheads and distant peaks were sublime, but the mountains could also be a place of potentially harsh, life-threatening experiences. Though I was grateful to have had this experience of climbing in the mountains with Chuck, I realized that what I enjoyed most of all was rock climbing. Exploring a sense of movement on the rocks, without risking life and limb in the death zone, was where I placed my destiny. I didn't feel the need to court death in order to get meaning from climbing, I decided.

One form of climbing that suited my interests more closely was "bouldering." When Chuck introduced me to this form of climbing on the boulders that are scattered on the desert floor of Joshua Tree, I discovered the heart of free climbing movement in its purest form.

Surrounding the campgrounds were scores of boulders that offered mini-climbs just a few feet tall but of extreme difficulty. They were so short that no rope was needed. Clans of climbers would wander through these boulder fields, working on "problems," where they'd climb a few feet up a boulder, try a move, then jump or fall off. After a short rest they'd try the problem again, but this time they'd be armed with more information about the climb and would more efficiently swing into the sequence of moves they'd perfected on the last try, getting a little farther. I saw similarities between the choreographing of moves in bouldering and those I had been taught for performing gymnastic routines. Both disciplines even depended on a "spotter" to catch one's mistakes. But where gymnastics required a contrived, scripted form of grace, climbing was beautifully free-form and spontaneous, each movement being different from any other.

When I saw a photo of John Gill hanging from an overhanging face by his fingertips, I was amazed to see how he was able to transfer his gymnastics skills on the rock. Having been a competitive rope climber, Gill was as famous for his incredible strength and technique as he was for his acrobatic leaps up the rock. A visionary climber who was ahead of his times, Gill did the first ascents of many difficult boulder problems across the country back in the late fifties—some of which weren't repeated for twenty-five years and others that are still unrepeated.

In delving into bouldering, I found that it wasn't much help to me to watch the way other climbers solved a problem. Being small, with my own unique physical characteristics, I found that I often climbed completely differently from the men who surrounded me. To get up a boulder problem, I had to explore all the options and touch all the holds myself. One day, I quickly made it to the top of a boulder problem called the Stem Gem by spanning across the rock with my flexible hips. When I reached the top and looked down, I noticed a male climber had been watching me.

"Gee, I can't even do that," he said dismissively, and walked off in a huff.

As I watched him walk away through the desert, I wondered about his remark and found myself taking it negatively. He could have commended me on succeeding on a climb that he could not do, but instead he seemed to brush it off as a bit of beginner's luck on my part. His assumption seemed to be that as a man he should automatically be physically superior to a small girl, and he seemed put out to see the "weaker sex" outdo him.

I was often disappointed by sexist attitudes outside the climbing

Using pretzel logic on the Stem Gem boulder, Joshua Tree. (JIM BRIDWELL)

scene, but it made me even more annoyed to see them among climbers. Perhaps this was because I felt that climbing was the first truly egalitarian activity I had participated in: everyone was equal before the rocks, it seemed to me. The beauty of climbing is that each person is free to choreograph his or her own way of adapting to the rock.

In fact, the very first climb I did at Joshua Tree, with Kathy, had been a fiasco because of stereotypical role playing. In an echo of that first day at Big Rock, Chuck chose a climb for us—a very easy route called Southeast Corner on Intersection Rock—and headed off elsewhere to climb with Bob. He expected Kathy to lead me up the route, and she let him think she was comfortable with that. But as before, as soon as Chuck was out of sight, Kathy suggested I lead. She wanted no part of the scary job of going first, placing the gear and mastering the moves. It seemed to me that Kathy was just humoring Chuck when it came to climbing. It was clear to me that Kathy came along not because she loved to climb, but because that was how Chuck wanted to spend their weekends.

When Kathy handed me the rack of gear for Southeast Corner, I barely knew what to do with it. Jangling around my neck was an array of about twenty gadgets, each on a sling of rope or wire, and each connected to my equipment sling that I had looped around my neck and shoulders. There were stoppers, which were V-shaped tapered wedges in a range of sizes from as thick as a wallet to as thin as a car key. They slotted into tapering pockets or cracks. Harder to figure out were the hexentrics, six-sided tubes of aluminum that at their biggest were the size of a clenched fist, and which had to be fiddled into a crack with more precision. Kathy proceeded to explain where the route went.

"Just climb up this short face to that flake up there. Once you get there, you can put one of those chocks into the crack," she said.

"What crack?" I asked.

"It's behind the flake. You can't see it from here, but you'll see it once you get there."

As I started up the route, I felt like a student pilot who'd just signed up for flight school and was unexpectedly handed the controls of a plane. I padded up a low-angle slab of rock for several feet, then looked back down toward the ground. When I realized that a fall meant that I would land quite a long way down on some big boulders, I felt the sting of adrenaline in the pit of my stomach. Suddenly I felt completely ill-prepared to continue upward.

"How do I use these things anyway?" I said, referring to the collection of gear I was carrying.

"You just place them in the crack wherever there's a constriction. You'll see, they work really well."

"But what happens if I fall here?"

"I don't know. Just don't fall, okay?"

Chuck had a sort of mantra about climbing: "The leader never falls." This ethic was reminiscent of the early days in climbing, at a time when there were no stoppers or hexentrics at all, and if you did fall you'd probably be pulverized on the ground below. I knew that Chuck and everyone else did suffer falls from time to time, so I took it to mean that you can only afford to fall if you have properly placed protection in the rock.

I looked around me and realized that I was out of my league. Though I was eager to climb, I wasn't willing to run blindly into something I was clueless about.

"I'm not doing this. I'm coming back down," I said.

"All right, then, come down."

Kathy seemed glad. When I reversed my moves and stepped onto the ground, she happily packed up our gear and led the way back to camp. I, on the other hand, felt cheated out of a day of action on the rock and kept thinking about what I could have done to make the climb a success. When Kathy saw the look of disappointment on my face, she offered condolences.

"Oh, don't feel bad. I tell you what, let's just tell Chuck that we didn't do the climb because you felt sick."

My mouth gaped. Did we really need an excuse? Couldn't we tell the truth, which was that one of us didn't really want to climb because she only does it to humor her boyfriend, and the other is too clueless to lead? Kathy seemed to assume Chuck would be disappointed that we hadn't done a climb, and she didn't want to let him down. Exploiting some kind of feminine weakness—"the girl got sick, and you know how girls get sick"—was just a device to appease Chuck.

I had seen this sort of game before, with our parents. On a surfing weekend to Huntington Beach, an argument between Mom and Dad over some trivial matter had been settled by Mom when she quipped, "Okay, Jim, you're right." To her, it seemed less important whether she was right or wrong. What mattered more was to keep the peace, even if it meant capitulating to her husband. This attitude left me a little dumbfounded. Was this what women were expected to do?

But these were carefree days. I was competing on the high school gymnastics team, so my weekdays were taken up with training and school, while my weekends and school breaks were devoted to climbing. I thought about climbing day in and day out. At night as I lay in bed, I would envision myself on future climbs on the big walls of Yosemite, Joshua Tree, or Tahquitz Rock, and I would soon feel my palms sweating with excitement.

Then, in the fall of 1976, the solid foundation of our family that I had always taken for granted was shattered by a devastating event. I learned of this disaster one evening after dinner when my brother Jim and I were sitting along the edge of the brick walkway in front of the house. I didn't suspect anything was wrong, when all of a sudden Jim said, "Mom and Dad are having serious marital problems."

"What do you mean?"

"Dad has a girlfriend."

"How do you know that?"

"Dad told me."

I was stunned. I had no idea that anything was amiss in my parents' relationship. If anything, they seemed like the perfect couple. They'd been together for twenty years. Relatively young, physically and intellectually alive, they socialized with a group of friends in the neighborhood, and they appeared to be happy together. If they argued, they did it so that I barely noticed a word out of place between them. Later, as an adult, I understood how this could happen, but at this time I took the news with utter astonishment.

Jim revealed that Dad had taken each of the "big kids" to dinner, separately, to break the news. Jim, being the oldest son, had heard more details about the situation than anyone else had. Instead of sympathizing with his father, he had become quite upset. Us "little kids" learned of this shocking news from our older siblings.

"Who is she?" I asked, suddenly feeling as curious as I felt shocked.

I learned that my father's new love was half his age and that she lived in Texas and worked in a bar. They had met when Dad had gone to Houston on business. Further snippets of information that Jim and my other brothers and sisters would learn formed a rough picture: she had a southern accent; she studied architecture and French; she had a big smile.

"How do you think Mom is taking this?" I wanted to know.

"She's very upset and angry with him. But mostly she just wants him to think it over carefully and not do anything rash," Jim said.

During the next few weeks a strange, uncomfortable undercurrent ran through the Hill family. Dad remained part of the household, yet he was withdrawn. We all did our best to carry on with our daily lives, but no one dared to broach the issue directly with our parents. They issued few announcements regarding the status of their impending separation. Whatever I gleaned about it filtered in to me as if my senses were absorbing the news but my mind wasn't. All of us held on to the hope that Dad would change his mind and stay.

Mom held on stoically, though as time passed she shed a great deal of weight. One night, as my mother and I piled the dishes from the evening meal into the sink, I saw that she was staring abstractedly at the plates. Then she began to weep.

"Doesn't it bother you, what's going on?" she asked, wiping her eyes.

It bothered me immensely, yet I felt powerless to do anything about the situation. These matters had been shaped by adults and I was a teenager. I didn't know what to say or do other than to hug my mother and cry. I felt a terrible sadness for her, and was aware that she faced the prospect of beginning a new way of life as a single mother with four children still under the age of eighteen. The situation seemed like a nightmare that I hoped we would all wake from soon.

Then came the dark Christmas of 1976, the last Christmas my father spent with us all together. No one had planned that Dad should spend Christmas with us, but December came around and before we knew it a Christmas tree sat in our living room like an unwelcome guest. We went through the motions of exchanging gifts and cards, but no one's heart was in it. The tension between what we felt and what we were acting out pushed all the joy from the room. There was no longer any denying that our family had changed forever.

And then Dad was gone.

For me, it was a confusing period with much sadness and uncertainty. Gradually, the climbing life I was discovering supplanted the family life that was crumbling all around me. There was only one way to handle the meltdown of our family: by quietly accepting it as proof that nothing in life is permanent. I looked to my weekend excursions to Joshua Tree as a life raft, and the act of climbing as therapy. To this day, climbing is still one of the few activities that makes me feel good even when I'm feeling down.

Chapter 4

Joshua Tree

The band of residents who were establishing the routes at Joshua Tree kept to themselves and looked upon people outside their circle, like Chuck and our group, with skepticism. While Chuck respected the superior abilities of those climbers, he saw in them no small amount of arrogance. To this end, he and Bob called the good climbers the "Haughties," for their haughty attitude. Conveniently, the term sounded a lot like the "Hotties," and "hot"—or talented—they certainly were.

The origins of this name came from an encounter with one of the local "Haughties" in Joshua Tree one day. It concerned one of the best of that bunch, a ripped, blond Adonis named John Bachar. Bachar had developed a head for climbing routes of great difficulty without a rope—an activity known as free soloing. It was immensely exciting to watch a climber carefully yet confidently climb a route without a rope. Today I would say that soloing is a case of so much to lose, so little to gain, in that the fleeting sense of personal satisfaction in the experience must be outweighed by the risk of death or broken limbs if the climber falls to the ground. Yet Bachar was a solo maestro, and he never put the wrong foot forward when free soloing.

After watching Bachar solo a route rated 5.11 called Left Ski Track, Chuck, Bob, and I waited until he had scrambled down the easy descent. Chuck expressed his admiration by simply exclaiming, "That was hot!"

Bachar strode by, barely even looking at us, and as he sauntered off among the boulders he sniggered in mimicry of Chuck, "Yeah, hot! Real hot!"

Hence the "Haughties."

One day I unwittingly gave the Haughties a good show on a route called EBGB's, whose name is a pun on two things, one being the slang expression for your nerves when scared—the "heebie-jeebies"—and the other being a corruption of the famous New York nightclub CBGB's. Chuck had given the route a try but had failed to make it past the first hard move, so he handed the lead over to me. As I started up the route, I began to appreciate Chuck's old adage that "the leader never falls" because EBGB's involved long sections of hard climbing between the bolts. Unbeknownst to me, a few of the Haughties were watching from a distance to see if little Lynnie might "take a whipper."

I started out on the route strongly, quickly overcoming the move that had stumped Chuck. That move was easier for me due to my small size and flexibility. It involved a "mantel" move, which is best described by a mental vision: imagine the movements one's body would be put through if one had to climb up and stand on the mantelpiece over the living room fireplace. On EBGB's I was able pull up to chest height on a shelf of rock, then pivot my hands and elbows around and press down until both arms were in a straight-locked position. I then swung my foot up to waist level next to my hands and stood up. At that point I realized I had gotten in over my head.

The moves above me involved gripping tiny flakes with my fingertips, move after move, for fifty feet. "Crimping," as this sort of finger-bending climbing is known, creates a painful "pump," or buildup of fatigue in the forearms. The farther I went, the more I felt I might fly off backward. A high of adrenaline began to spur me on. As I eyed the last move onto the top of the dome, I thought, *Ahh, the top at last.* I began to make a high step onto a shallow, sloping depression on the face, and as I shifted my weight, my foot slipped off and I toppled over backward. Thirty feet later, I bounced onto the rope and hung upside down in my harness. Dazed but unscathed, I righted myself and lowered off. It would be a couple more years before I had the courage to try this climb again, but the show I had given the Haughties earned me an invitation.

Not long after, one of the most endearing of the Haughties visited our campsite at breakfast time. His name was John Long, and his nickname reflected his bodybuilder dimensions—*largo* being Spanish for "large." Largo hailed from Claremont, California, and was in the process of perfecting his own power-based style of climbing in which he

John Long on the Pinch Grip Overhang in Horsetooth Reservoir, Colorado. (MICHAEL KENNEDY)

would fling himself up difficult sections of rock by dynamically pro-
pelling his body upward with a mighty pull of his arms. But what set
him apart was his blustering attitude and his mastery of the campfire
scene, where he held court by telling jokes, impossibly tall tales, and
even reciting self-penned poems in his loud baritone voice.

John had been on his way out to go climbing with his friends when
he spotted me from across the campground and said, "Hold on. Let's
ask that girl over there to come with us."

Then he jogged over to our campsite and promptly asked, "We're on
our way out to try a new route called the Equinox today. Do you want
to join us?"

Although I wasn't sure what I would be getting into, I didn't hesitate
one minute to spend the day with a group of climbers who were, at the
time, the best in the country.

Billy Westbay, Jim
Bridwell, and John
Long after the first
one-day ascent of the
Nose. (JIM BRIDWELL
COLLECTION)

After that first day of climbing with John Long on the Equinox, I was accepted into the group of pranksters, eccentrics, and savants that I had previously known only as the Haughties. That day John coined his own nickname for me, "Little Herc," since he said I looked as strong as Hercules. What began as a small group of friends expanded into a community of people from all walks of life. Quite a few were students majoring in esoteric fields like astrophysics, math, and archaeology. There were also a lot of unemployed vagabonds, and even a few whose lives hovered on the fringe of legality. But most of the climbers I knew held down an array of jobs and careers from carpenters and construction workers to doctors, lawyers, scientists, actors, and shop managers. Climbing was the one passion we all shared in common.

Chief of the Haughties was Largo, with his blustering yet sweet omnipresence and his weight-training-fueled climbing strength. Largo had recently participated in one of the major events in American climbing: the first one-day ascent of the Nose route on El Capitan in Yosemite Valley. Normally, this 3,000-foot route took climbers several days to climb, but when Largo, Jim Bridwell, and Billy Westbay teamed up and blitzed it in a fifteen-hour marathon in the summer of 1975, it shattered the previous standards of athletic performance on the rock.

Largo was also a founding member of that unofficial clan of climbers known as the Stonemasters, a loose collective of incredibly fit, daring, and talented Californians who led the world in rock climbing during the seventies. The name said it all: mastery over the stone, and mastery over being stoned. It was an elite club that had no admission fees, charter, or secret handshake, but this clan was exclusively male and a ritual was required to join. Initiation as a Stonemaster came from making one of the first ten ascents of Valhalla, a particularly tricky and scary route on the granite cliff of Suicide Rocks in the San Jacinto Mountains above Idyllwild. The climb—first ascended by Bud "Ivan" Couch—had such an epic reputation with the young climbers of the day that mastery over it had become a rite of passage, a bit like the moment when a young Indian brings down his first buffalo.

Years later I heard the story about how Maria Cranor did an on-sight ascent of Valhalla after her partners, Kevin Powell, Tim Powell, and Darrel Hensel, failed to lead the route. (An "on-sight" ascent is particularly impressive in that a climber free climbs the route without a fall, having never practiced or seen the moves before.) Meanwhile, Mari Gingery and John Long were at the top of Insomnia Crack watching as she cruised up the first two pitches. When Maria arrived at the belay before the last pitch and said she wanted to descend, John shouted to her, "No, you must keep going!" So Maria continued up and made not only the first ascent by a woman but she made a perfect on-sight ascent, back in 1978!

Nearly everyone in the climbing scene sported a nickname. Russ Walling, the Fish, was so named because he liked to fake flipping, twitching epileptic fits in front of tourists. Out of this he got pity, spare change, or, if he grossed out the tourists and they abandoned their picnic, he got a crack at their sandwiches. Bullwinkle, a.k.a. Dean Fidelman, was, and remains today, a photographer. For two decades Dean has documented many classic moments out at the crags through his black-and-white photography.

Dave Neilson, Too Tall, at nearly six feet four inches, could easily reach holds on climbs that most of us had to jump to. Tobin Sorenson had no particular nickname, but he had a presence. A modest person, he bundled within his climbing persona a weird blend of skill and clumsiness, athletic drive and recklessness, boldness and Christianity. He was polite, and painfully shy around women. When most climbers would scream, "Oh, shit," in terror whenever they fell off, Tobin would demurely quip, "Oh, biscuit," and he fell regularly and far because he was into pushing his limits in order to push the frontier of climbing. His fearlessness seemed in part born out of a religious background. After he disappeared from the climbing scene for a few months, he returned with tales of smuggling Bibles into communist Bulgaria. Later, after he had immersed himself in mountaineering, I saw a grinning magazine photo of him on Switzerland's dangerous Eiger North Wall. On his helmet he had written "One Way" with an arrow pointing heavenward.

By day we climbed, by night we played. The maze of canyons and boulders around Joshua Tree provided a fine natural playground for après-climb activities. Moonlight ascents were among our favorite pastimes. On these nocturnal excursions we'd wander out through the desert to some easy dome of rock, dodging cholla cactus and the spiny bayonets of yucca trees as we came on them in the dark. Then, as agile as raccoons, we'd scamper up and down under the lunar light. On those moonlit nights coyotes would howl crazily in the distance. On darker nights we watched shooting stars, and distant pinpoints of light that were probably military missions flying around the Twenty-nine Palms Marine base. And J-Tree was reminiscent of the mysterious site called Area 51, where supermarket tabloids and TV shows had claimed for three decades that an alien spacecraft had crashed. Such stories postulated that a top-secret desert lab was trying to replicate the craft and master the art of flying it. Such fantastic stuff appealed to us and we'd study each speck of light, imagining it to be a spaceship coming to take us on the ultimate adventure. Always there to ground us back to reality was the pulsing orb of Los Angeles not far beyond the horizon.

Among the more outrageous of my new friends was John Yablonsky. Going by the nickname of Yabo, this twenty-year-old had recently dropped out of high school and left his unhappy home to become a denizen of Joshua Tree by winter and Yosemite Valley by summer. He had little shape to his life except what climbing offered it, yet in that arena he excelled. Otherwise he was rarely employed, more rarely washed, and perpetually penniless. With an untidy mop of dark blond hair, Yabo resembled the Artful Dodger in Charles Dickens's *Oliver Twist*. He went by numerous other titles: the Yarbarian was one. A loner by nature, he liked to joke that he was the sole member of a one-man tribe, and that tribe he dubbed the Yabaho Tribe. Though I found it strange to be around him when he uttered his nervous, staccato laugh and began hammering on an empty tin can to produce the bongo-driven, ritual-sounding chant of the Yabaho Tribe, I nevertheless felt a sense of compassion for Yabo.

One night the crowd put down a stake of $5 to dare Yabo to make a nude moonlight solo of a route named North Overhang. The route is rated 5.9, and its trickiest section requires one to climb a section of a crack splitting through a nearly horizontal ceiling of rock. Not having a penny to his name, Yabo unhesitatingly took the meager bet, stripped, and set off up the climb clad only in rock shoes, a chalk bag, and a wool cap. Those on the ground heckled him as he swung baboonlike through the roof, and we shone our flashlights onto his bare, untanned rump. When he finished the climb, he down-climbed the other side of the overhang and returned to the ground, only to find that his clothes had been snatched and hidden by one of his friends. We laughed while he wandered stark naked in the cold desert air for a few minutes, but then he reached under a rock and pulled out another set of trousers, socks, and a sweater.

"I might be crazy, but I'm no fool," he said, cackling the deranged laugh I would grow to know well in the coming years. Yabo had predicted his scurrilous companions would take advantage of him and spirit his clothes away, so he'd quietly stashed a spare set just in case.

More often than not, campfires were dominated by Largo's boisterous tale-telling. While flames animated our shadows against a backdrop of Volkswagen vans and rusting jalopies, Largo would recount fabulous stories that were half true and half a cocktail of imagination. He was a born raconteur with not a trace of shyness in him, and Largo's 205-pound frame roved the fringe of the campfire as if it were a stage and he the main event. The most memorable tale I heard him tell concerned a hair-raising experience during a day when he was soloing routes at J-Tree, trying to keep up with John Bachar. Largo was a formidable climber in his own right, but he held Bachar's free soloing ability in high esteem.

"All climbs are easy for Bachar," he said. "He completely dominates the cliff with his grace and confidence. He never rattles, never loses control."

Bachar and a few others had developed a sort of high-stakes cult in which they would solo route after route, sometimes at levels as demanding as 5.12. The subsport of soloing rock climbs even hit the media's radar when in the early eighties *Newsweek* ran a story about Bachar's ropeless exploits.

Largo's tale began with him arriving in J-Tree during a spring break from college. A meeting with Bachar leads to a darelike invitation to embark on a soloing tour. Being the host, Bachar offers Largo a choice: they could have an "El Cap day" or a "Half Dome day." El Cap is 3,000 feet tall, which translates into climbing about thirty pitches. Half Dome is 2,000 feet, which equals about twenty pitches. All unroped. Largo wisely chooses the Half Dome option.

"In a wink Bachar was booted up and he set off," Largo told the campfire crowd. "He climbed flawlessly, then it was my turn to solo up behind him. I was nervous as hell. Shaking. As if jackals were running up and down my spine."

**John Bachar free solo-
ing Leave It To Beaver
(5.12).** (JOHN BACHAR COL-
LECTION)

Their method was to climb a hard route on a particular formation
about 150 feet tall, then they'd descend via a different, easy route. After
three hours they'd disposed of a dozen climbs.

"We felt invincible," Largo decreed. "Then we upped the ante from
easy 5.9 to a stiff 5.10. Now we were in expert terrain. We slowed
down, but by early afternoon we'd climbed our twenty pitches. Half
Dome was history."

But there was still daylight and Bachar suggested they solo a 5.11—
a tough feat even for Bachar. Listening to Largo describe what came
next left me slack-mouthed and awed.

Largo described how Bachar escorted him to Intersection Rock, to
the climb where Chuck, Bob, and I had watched Bachar free solo Left
Ski Track. Scores of climbers from all over the world "froze like stat-
ues" when Bachar started up unroped.

"He moved with flawless precision, plugging his fingertips into shallow pockets in the hundred-and-five-degree wall. I scrutinized his moves, making mental notes on the intricate sequence. He paused at 50 feet, directly below the crux bulge. Splaying his left foot out onto a slanting edge, he pinched a tiny rib and pulled through to a gigantic bucket hold. Then he walked up the last 100 feet of vertical rock like a kid climbing a staircase. From the summit Bachar flashed down that sly, candid snicker."

Largo told how he headed up.

"The first bit passed quickly. Everything was clicking along, severe but steady. Then I glided into the coffin zone," he said.

This sinister-sounding zone was a bit of Largo-speak, like Messner's "death zone" in the Himalayas. Simply put, it represented the point on a solo climb above 50 feet. Fall from there, and you'd probably end up in a wooden box.

Largo now had the campfire crowd in the palm of his hand. He turned up the drama, describing in animated detail how he bungled a sequence of moves while deep in the coffin zone.

"Man, my hands were too low to reach up for the big 'Thank God' bucket hold just above me, and my puny power was going fast. My foot started vibrating and I was instantly desperate, wondering if and when my body would plummet. There was no reversing any of this because you can't down-climb truly hard rock any more than a hurdler can run the one-ten 'highs' backward. The only way off was up. A montage of black images flooded my brain."

As Largo described the climb of his life, flickering campfire flames enhanced his stage movements. He contorted himself into the position that he had climbed himself into on that route—a position that he could not move out of.

"I was stuck, terrified, my whole existence focused down to a pin-point, a single move. Arms shot, legs wobbling, head on fire. Then my fear overwhelmed itself and a little voice calmly intoned, 'At least die trying.'"

Largo then demonstrated to the crowd the muscle-twisting maneuver he pulled off to get himself out of the jam he was in. A nanosecond before his strength evaporated and he would free-fall to oblivion, he summoned all his remaining adrenaline and heaved through a do-or-die maneuver. When he grabbed the bucket hold and pulled onto the easier climbing above it, he stood quaking on the rock. He didn't want to go any higher—"I'd rather yank my wisdom teeth with Vise-Grips than continue up," he said. But he had to keep going. As he clawed up the last hundred feet, dancing black orbs dotted his vision, a residue from the onslaught of fear and adrenaline. On top Bachar snickered and told Largo that he had "looked a little shaky."

"The next day I didn't climb," Largo confessed. "Instead I wandered listlessly through dark desert corridors, scouting for turtles, making garlands of wildflowers, relishing the skyscape, doing all those things a person does on borrowed time."

Years later he would pen the story of this climb and call it "The Only Blasphemy." It would become one of the classics of climbing writing. In that tale, of the pivotal moment of risk recognition when he was poised between life and death, he wrote: "Shamefully I understood that the only blasphemy was to willfully jeopardize my own existence."

Most campfire yarns portrayed brinkmanship as a virtue. They were exciting, scary, and funny. They always ended on a happy I-made-it-by-the-skin-of-my-teeth note. We were all still young back then and mortality had yet to track us down.

Another riotous Largo campfire thriller, later published as a story called "Three Little Fish," concerned Tobin's first ascent of a climb at Tahquitz Rock, a climb named the Green Arch. This climb was the focus of several attempts by the Stonemasters, but every time they tried its smooth wall and its leaning open-book-shaped corner, they would be spat out. Only Largo had gotten high enough in the corner to gingerly touch the rounded mushroom-shaped knobs of dark rock on the wall above. He pronounced them as being ungrippable and he continued shuffling across the leaning arch until fatigue made him sag onto a piton he had laboriously hammered into the crack. Largo lowered back to the ground. It was now Tobin's turn to try. He immediately climbed up to the ungrippable knobs.

"No, those knobs don't go anywhere," Largo yelled, but it was too late.

"Understand that Tobin was a born-again Christian, that he'd smuggled Bibles into Bulgaria risking twenty-five years on a Balkan rock pile, that he'd studied God at a fundamentalist university," Largo explained. "And understand that Tobin was perfectly mad. Out on the sharp end he ignored all consequences. He even mocked them. Once, at Joshua Tree, I saw him climb a difficult crack with a noose tied around his neck. But most horrifying was his capacity to charge at a climb pell-mell."

Largo described how on straightforward routes Tobin's charge was an impressive display, but on routes requiring patience and cunning he was a disaster and he would climb into the most grievous predicaments.

"Against all my advice, Tobin clawed his way up to that sea of knobs. Just as I predicted, it was a dead end and he was stuck. The full impact of his folly hit him like a wrecking ball. He panicked and wailed and nearly wept," said Largo.

Tobin was 25 feet from the piton, so if he fell he would fall that distance, plus the 25 feet past the piton. There would be rope stretch and slack in the belay to add another 10 feet. But, as Largo pointed out, the chances were that the lousy blade-shaped piton he had bashed into the crack under the roof would rip out under the force of a fall. He would then drop a further 20 feet to the next piece of gear, making for an 80-foot fall. Largo worried that Tobin would end up crashing into the ground.

"As Tobin wobbled far overhead, who should lumber up to our little group but his very father—a minister, and a quiet, retiring, imperturbable gentleman who hacked and huffed from his long march up to the cliff. After hearing so much about climbing from Tobin, he'd finally come to see his son in action."

The sweat-soaked, mustached pastor "squinted up at the fruit of his loins." Tobin's knees knocked like castanets and he sobbed pitifully at the prospect of his fall. Then he suddenly screamed down to Largo, "I'm gonna jump."

"Jump off?"

"Yes!"

"No!" Largo screamed.

"You can do it, son," the pastor put in.

Inspired by his father's urging, Tobin groped at the holds above, but his fate was sealed. A second later he came flying off the wall. The top piton ripped out with a pinging sound. He screamed. His arms flailed as he cartwheeled through the air. Then the lower piton caught him and he jolted to a stop. Largo lowered him to the ground, where he lay motionless, moaning softly.

"He had a lump the size of a pot roast over one eye. Then he wobbled to his feet," said Largo.

"I'll get it next time," Tobin grumbled.

"There ain't gonna be a next time," declared Richard.

"Give the boy a chance," the pastor put in, thumping Tobin on the back.

This proved to Largo that both father and son were mad, and they withdrew for the day. The first ascent of the Green Arch finally came four years later, when Rick Accomazzo led it in a bold brilliant stroke. Largo and Tobin followed on the rope. Tobin went on to the European Alps to solo the north face of the Matterhorn, the Walker Spur, and the Shroud on the Grandes Jorasses, and he made the first alpine-style ascent of the direct route on the Eiger. I had read of these climbs in Chuck's apartment, particularly the latter, on which the American climber John Harlin had fallen thousands of feet to his death after a rope snapped. Tobin's list of solo mountain climbs grew as the years rolled on, and he became one of America's most famous alpinists. Then he met his end in the Canadian Rockies in 1980.

Largo wrote something of an obituary for his friend and in it he said, "I've never since experienced the electricity of watching Tobin out there on the quick of the long plank, clawing for the promised land. He finally found it while attempting a solo ascent of Mount Alberta's north face. His death was a tragedy. But I sometimes wonder if God himself could no longer bear the strain of watching Tobin wobbling and lunging way out there on the sharp end of the rope, and finally just drew him into the fold."

During my last year in high school, I found myself examining the concrete jungle of our LA environment with a sense of detachment. More and more I came to believe that my sense of belonging was with the imperfect family of friends I was meeting in the climbing scene. From that point on, I drifted away from climbing with Chuck, Kathy, and Bob. The change came as a natural transition for all of us. It was as if we each had our own separate paths to follow. I was reminded of the poignant prediction my brother Jim had made on our family outing years earlier: "You know, one day when we're all grown up, we'll have

Bachar trying to impress us with his long-jumping skills, in camp at J-Tree. From left to right, Mari Gingery, Jessica Perrin, Roy McClenahan, Rick Cashner, John Long, me (hidden), and John Bachar. (DEAN FIDELMAN)

families of our own and we won't live together anymore." Chuck's jaunts to Joshua Tree became fewer as his interests shifted more to mountaineering and less to rock climbing. As for Kathy, she became immersed in her pharmacology studies at the University of Southern California and in working part-time. Bob continued to climb easy routes in the mountains with Chuck, but his outings on the rock became less frequent as his time was taken up with work and studying psychology at Fullerton Junior College. As for me, I felt a calling coming from the rocky places like Joshua Tree. There, I felt as if I were a welcome figure in a familiar landscape.

Chapter 5

White Wind

Kathy tells a story about the moment in January 1980 when she had a premonition that Chuck had died. She was winter camping in Yosemite and a blizzard was raging outside the tent. All through the night she and her tent mate had to dig their tent out from a growing weight of snow to keep it from collapsing. Kathy lay in the tent shivering, drifting in and out of a troubled sleep. A sense of Chuck filled her thoughts. In those images he was in dire trouble. In reality, Chuck was, at that moment, fighting for his life somewhere around 22,000 feet on Aconcagua, the tallest peak on the South American continent. A month earlier he had followed his own mountaineering dream and had joined an expedition to attempt the first American ascent of the mountain's enormous and dangerous south face.

Chuck and Kathy had married in August 1977, after an eight-year courtship. Initially the marriage had gone well, but Chuck's decision to stop teaching high school geography and devote his time to being in the mountains meant he saw less of Kathy and they began to drift apart. By the middle of 1979 they were separated, and Chuck took the split badly. I remember a weekend when I found myself in Yosemite Valley at the same time as Chuck, and I chanced upon him sitting in his car, tearfully writing a letter to Kathy. Chuck was quietly devastated by the failure of his marriage, yet, perhaps strangely, after he moved out of the apartment that he and Kathy had shared, he maintained his link to the Hill family by moving into my brother Bob's apartment in Fullerton. As is often the case with men who climb and who have suffered an emotional trauma like a marital breakup, he found solace by devoting himself to climbing more seriously than ever before. Perhaps he was casting off the last shred of stability that a mate provides by plunging into the uncertainty of adventure.

Aconcagua is an ancient volcano 22,834 feet high in the Andes of southern Argentina. Though gigantic, from most views it is an unattractive peak, a hump, really, made of a dirty jumble of ash-smeared glaciers and decaying rock. If not for the fact that it is the highest point in South America, few people would bother to trudge up its gently angled north and east flanks. But Aconcagua's status as the highest on the continent gives it enough caché to attract hundreds of mountaineers from all over the world each year. It is even likely that ancient Incans climbed the mountain; a mummy was dug up at 17,800 feet. The first Westerners to climb it came in 1897, under the guiding eye of the Swiss mountaineer Matthias Zurbriggen. That ascent was from the north.

Ascents of the northern or eastern sides require only high-altitude walking. As of today, mountain bikes and dogs have even made it to the summit via the northern route, but nevertheless by 1979 some two hundred climbers had died while trying to get up, or down, those "easy" routes. High-altitude cerebral edema and pulmonary edema accounted for a good share of those deaths, but the real killer on Aconcagua is the wind. Known as El Viento Blanco, or the White Wind, it is a maelstrom that originates in Antarctica, races across the southern oceans and the Argentinean pampas, and slams into the exposed heights of Aconcagua at speeds in excess of a hundred miles per hour. In the arid cold found at the tallest reaches, El Viento Blanco produces temperatures capable of freezing flesh or inducing hypothermia in minutes. Such a wind can pin a climber to the mountainside and make movement impossible. If it blows fast enough, it can even suck the atmosphere from around the mountain and leave pockets where there is barely enough oxygen to breathe. The trick to surviving such hostile elements is to climb the mountain as fast as possible. This makes the easy north and east flanks the most viable gamble.

But it was not the easy way up that Chuck and his companions had in mind. From the south, Aconcagua presents an entirely different picture. Rising from the Horcones Glacier, the south face is a 10,000-foot precipice of rotten rock towers, gaping cold chimneys, and collapsing ice cliffs. The first party to climb it, in 1954, was a six-man French expedition led by René Ferlet. The climbers worked on their route for a month, weaving a path around steep rock towers and ice cliffs that frequently avalanched. During that month they set up a series of well-supplied camps linked together with thousands of feet of rope. When they were within striking distance of the summit, they set out for a final climb that ended up lasting seven days. On the last day a storm battered them, nearly freezing them to the face. They continued up, but by the time they descended from the summit, all of the climbers had frostbite. Back in France, only one of the climbers avoided amputations of fingers and toes. Ever after, the south face of Aconcagua—an ancient Incan word meaning "sentinel of stone"—has been shrouded in notoriety among climbers.

Between the French expedition and 1979, a mere six expeditions had claimed success over this intimidating wall. None of the victors were American. That distinction attracted the leader of Chuck's expedition, thirty-seven-year-old Ed Connor, a civil engineer and builder of golf courses who lived in Palm Springs, California. The kudos of having a tough "first" under one's belt is an integral part of the climbing experience, and Aconcagua from the south was a worthy objective to satisfy such an ambition. Connor started climbing comparatively late in life, when he was thirty. He had extensive experience on hard ice climbs and multiday rock climbs and had climbed a few mountains, but most of what he had done was in the league of high-altitude, nontechnical snow climbs. He made an ascent of Mount McKinley (20,320 feet) in 1973 and Mount Orizaba (18,700 feet) in Mexico in 1977. His most ambi-

tious attempt on a mountain came in 1978, when he joined an expedition to Annapurna III (24,787 feet) in Nepal. Although this seven-man
team was unsuccessful in their attempt to climb a new route, the experience proved to be valuable on Aconcagua.

For Aconcagua, Connor asked along his partner from Annapurna,
twenty-year-old Guy Andrews, a San Diego travel agent. Andrews, a
bachelor, was a lean, physically strong youth with a natural climbing
talent. In his Aconcagua diary Connor wrote glowingly of his protégé:
"Guy will be one of the best. I can't even describe to him what is in
store for him if he continues at his present pace. Ideal job, good physical attributes. Good mental attitude. I only hope to contribute to his
development. He can be the Jack Nicklaus of climbing in a few years.
Another Messner."

Chuck appeared to be the odd man out on the team. He didn't really
know Connor or Andrews and he had never been higher than 14,000
feet on a mountain. He had heard through a mutual friend in their local
climbing community, Steve Van Meter, that Connor was financing
everything but air travel on an expedition to Aconcagua and that a
third member was needed, so he went to meet the other men at
Connor's house in Palm Springs. After a few practice climbs in nearby
Yosemite to test their compatibility, Connor invited Chuck to join the
expedition. Chuck was eager and willing to go, and he had the money.
Now that he was a bachelor again, he had the time. What he lacked was
high-altitude climbing experience.

Connor took on a paternal role in his leadership of the expedition,
calling Chuck and Guy his "boys." While in Santiago, Chile, on their
way to the mountains, Connor wrote in his journal, "I'd forgotten what
it was like to be young and impatient. Chuck and Guy are just two
forces of light energy bursting at the seams. Focusing intense bursts on
the nearest female shape, their rock and roll cassette tapes, each other
and their aged leader. It's difficult at times to get a moment of peace
and Mozart around their energy belts."

Connor's journal would become the only record of Chuck's last days.

Connor and his team planned to tackle the south face in highly ambi-
tious style. Ever since the French, all the teams that had succeeded on

the south face—Argentinean, Chilean, Austrian (a team that included Reinhold Messner), and Japanese—had used the tactic known variously as "expedition style" or "siege style." This method of going up and down a mountain repeatedly to secure the route with thousands of feet of rope creates a "safe" highway that can aid in either a head start when it comes time to sprint to the summit or a speedy escape route to lower camps when the weather turns bad. Along the way, tent camps stocked with food and supplies are placed at strategic intervals. This time-honored but heavy-handed mode of ascent involves a large team with lots of gear and requires weeks of preparation before a summit team can be sent up.

Connor didn't want to climb Aconcagua that way. He and the boys wanted to dispense with the path of ropes and in-situ camps and make a bare-bones ascent, going from the bottom to the top in one fast push, camping on the face wherever night fell, carrying only what they could cram into their backpacks. Incredibly, they would even go so light as to not take a tent, reasoning that there would be few places to pitch a tent on the steep south face. Instead, they'd sit on ledges in their sleeping bags.

This was "alpine-style" climbing at its boldest. This way of climbing mountains had become the more respected style of mountaineering in the 1970s, largely due to the example of Reinhold Messner, a brilliant climber who espoused climbing mountains "by fair means." Messner pooh-poohed the grand old style of big expeditions. Confronting the mountains in this lightweight manner was more adventuresome and more spiritually connected to the mountain, yet more risky and less certain of success. It was a style befitting only elite climbers.

The team landed in Santiago on December 15 and headed to Mendoza. They got along well from the start. "We really felt we were taking on a significant first; there was a real sense of adventure," Connor told an interviewer after the climb. "We felt pretty special. There was a lot of camaraderie. It showed. At the airports. At dinner together. We were a pretty close group."

A bus ride took the climbers and their six hundred pounds of supplies to Mendoza. The bulk of their gear jammed the bus, crowding the Argentine passengers, who jokingly called them *gringos locos*. To the local people it must have seemed strange that they had come so far for a holiday on frigid Aconcagua. From Mendoza another bus took them another hundred miles to the Puente del Inca ski hut at the end of the road. They rented mules to carry their loads and headed toward the mountain. Connor recorded in his journal their first view of the mountain:

> The Andes have the majestic allure of the Himalayas without the tropical climate at lower elevations. This tends to make the trekking much more pleasurable. The Horcones Valley has a stark beauty and grandeur I was unprepared for. Huge tilted strata of ancient sandstone stacked row upon row for your viewing pleasure. Because I now get away only once or twice a year or so, I think each experience is more enriching to me. The South Face is magnificent. One-and-a-half-times the face of the Eiger, four times Half Dome, with ice and altitude thrown in. Two-and-a-half-times El Cap. The scale is astonishing. There stands 10,000 feet of steep ice and rock and no American has climbed it! Unbelievable!

They placed a base camp at 13,000 feet and set about acclimatizing for the next twelve days. Connor, an amateur medical buff, monitored everyone's blood pressure, pulse rate, and lung capacity. He also tended to Chuck, who had developed serious diarrhea that they suspected was dysentery. After treatment with Lomotil and tetracycline antibiotics, Chuck felt better and joined Connor and Guy on short training climbs onto the lower ramparts of the mountain.

Timing of the ascent was a critical factor. After about a week in base camp to acclimate to the 12,000-foot elevation and venturing to around 16,000 feet on neighboring ridges during training with no ill effects, the team became concerned that the superb weather they had experienced might soon deteriorate.

Connor had directed a fair amount of attention to timing the size and location of the avalanches that seemed constantly to rack the face, adding to its menace. Connor wrote, "About 2:00 AM on the morning of Dec 30 a huge earthquake shook the area. Being from California, we all three knew at once what was happening. Our camp was safely away from any danger, but I stuck my head out of the tent in time to witness a spectacle never equaled in my experience. The entire 9 kilometer wide and 3 kilometer high South Face under a full moon started moving all at once in slow motion, as the Face shed millions of tons of unconsolidated snow and ice. It was mesmerizing to be standing within a mile of this event and to be so transfixed by it that thoughts of danger or fleeing didn't really occur to us. The spindrift settled to the bottom with a muffled roar that eventually cast a mild snow cloud over our camp with a gentle rustling of fabric. After the excitement subsided, we realized this was the sign we'd been waiting for. With the removal of all this unconsolidated material, we reckoned the avalanche danger would never be less than in the days following then earthquake."

So on New Year's Eve the three set off at four-thirty A.M. to start the climb. In each man's pack they carried gear and supplies weighing fifty pounds. That included food for six days. "There was an element of unpredictability about the climb," Connor said later. "We knew we were sticking our necks out farther than we ever had before. It intrigued us and gave us spirit to think that we could do the climb while realizing there was a possibility we couldn't. That's exactly where you want to be on a climb. If you were so certain of success, the spirit of adventure would be removed and you probably wouldn't even go to the effort."

The first day the trio strapped crampons to their boots and climbed 2,300 feet of snow to the bottom of a landmark on the face called the Broken Towers. To get there they had run a gauntlet of snowslides triggered by the morning sun, which warmed the slopes and set off avalanches. Higher up, bands of vertical ice cliffs, known as seracs, would also bust loose when warmed by the sun, sending tons of ice exploding down the mountain. The climbing route followed a winding path that narrowly avoided these hazards. At the Broken Towers their lives started getting difficult.

Wrote Connor, "We are on a knife-edge at 6:15 PM with no good bivouac ledges in sight. So we decide to find a better place to sleep. Chuck did a magnificent lead to get to the bivy but we lose! No ledge and no place to cook or lie flat. We bivy in an ice-filled chimney of rotten rock hanging in harnesses, unable to cook or sleep. The price we pay in loss of energy is at least a day."

When I learned that Chuck and his partners had stood upright all night, clipped to their harnesses to prevent them from slipping off the face, shivering, thirsty, and hungry because they could not set up a shelter or cook, it was obvious to me that from the very first day the odds were stacking up against them. To me, enduring such punishment and then continuing on up was hard to imagine. But carry on they did.

Again from Connor's journal: "Only reluctantly did the Towers release their hold on us. The last 20 feet we had to tiptoe on a knife edge arête with packs on and no belay. I just swallowed my apple, waiting for a death fall. My greatest fear now is that someone will make a tired mistake and we will have an accident."

After four hours of "struggling fearsomely," according to Connor, they reached the top of the Broken Towers. There they stopped to cook and rest. They didn't climb much farther, but stopped at a section known as the Sandstone Band. At the base of this 1,000-foot cliff they used their ice axes to chop out a ledge in the ice field and spent the night.

According to Connors, "I estimated we had surmounted the first third of the face (granted not the most difficult third). Although we did not find a great bivy site, the weather was good and we were not terribly uncomfortable. There was never any question of not continuing at this point. We were very fit and once we got some more snow melted at the top of the Broken Towers, we felt strong and confident."

The summit was visible above them. But how far above them they were unsure, as Connor couldn't be certain if his altimeter was reading the altitude correctly. It read 17,000 feet, yet he was certain they had climbed higher. But if the altimeter was right, they had nearly 6,000 feet remaining. Of his confusion over this Connor jotted down, "Nothing makes sense at this altitude . . . Surely we must be on Mars or at least the Moon, I feel mountain lassitude today. Dull, insipid thought patterns."

On day three they climbed with difficulty into the sandstone band, then an afternoon storm pelted them with snow. Connor took the lead and scurried about the rocky slope looking for a ledge they could squeeze their bodies onto for the night. Wrote Connor, "I promised Guy a flat place to lie down and so it shall be. I stamp out a flat place in the snow and bring the boys up. Both near hypothermia. We get settled about 9:00 PM. Dead tired and needing liquid and food badly. Force ourselves to cook and melt snow. Without liquid we will be wasted for the next day."

His journal records how the increased altitude made it hard to stomach their freeze-dried meal of shrimp creole, though they were famished. Then he wrote, "Guy develops a bad headache and numb feet. Chuck got snow-blind sometime this afternoon so we have to watch him. He is in great pain. Evening views from this space platform over the Central Andes are incredible. Unfortunately we were too concerned with survival to appreciate them."

Day four dawned fairly clear, but the drama, as carefully recorded by Connor, continued: "I lead off heading for a snow ramp and boom! My right leg disappears into a void. I look down into an evil hole about 10 feet wide with no bottom. I'm suspended by a rotten snow bridge. With Guy pulling me backward and a frantic ice ax arrest I'm able to roll back out of it. It does block the path to the ramp however, so I'm forced to do some rather desperate moves over a steep ice wall to get back onto the ramp. Very hard with a pack on!"

They camped in a small gully at the base of a section known as the French Rib. They were cooking dinner and trying to recover from the efforts of the day when a massive cliff of ice above them collapsed and set off an avalanche "big enough to bury 10 people." It missed them by 150 feet. "We are too tired to celebrate our good fortune," wrote Connor.

From this bivouac they hoped to get to the summit in one more day, but as it turned out, it took them three. They woke sluggish from altitude and from having been deluged by blowing spindrift, or powdery wind-blown snow that washes around the mountain like water. After taking a couple of hours to inventory their food and supplies and repack gear, they set off at ten-thirty A.M. Soon thereafter, Chuck stepped through a snowbridge partway into a crevasse and had to be pulled out. Connor was expecting to find somewhere on the rib above them an easy walk-off that headed over to the less steep summit plateau. But they found no escape route, only tricky rock pitches, all at around 20,500 feet.

"Chuck ignores his bout with snow blindness to push the lead about 60 or 70 feet," Connor wrote. "He gets stuck and Guy goes up to finish the pitch. In his haste to find us a decent bivy, Guy does not take enough gear and ends up getting stuck about 50 feet above Chuck. I holler for a retreat to the stance I'm on but they feel a good ledge is above."

Connor headed up toward them and realized quickly that they had a problem: both Guy and Chuck had left their packs with him and Connor could not drag three heavy packs up the wall. Darkness was falling and the wind building. Connor's journal then hinted at the stress that Chuck must have been feeling: "Chuck gets panicky and drops a glove which heightens his anxiety (and mine) . . . I pass him one of my own along with a sharp order for both men to GET DOWN NOW!!!"

Connor headed back down a few dozen feet to his belay ledge and began to chop at the ice to make a space for a bivouac. He ordered Guy to help Chuck get down, and he described Chuck as being "quite blown out by this time and I half expect to see him just plummet in his state of anxiety."

So Guy rappelled down the rope to Chuck and helped him regain his composure. The two of them descended to the three-by-four-foot ledge that Connor had been hacking away at. Said Connor later, "I would have hated to have seen Chuck try to come down without Guy's help because he was pretty panicked at this point. Sometimes you have to slap a guy and say, 'Hey, if you don't move from there you're gonna die.'"

In the middle of the night the dreaded El Viento Blanco rammed into them like a freight train. The three of them sat on a one-man ledge without a tent, with no room to even get in their sleeping bags, bearing the brunt of the freezing wind. Soon their feet began to grow colder and colder. Connor and Chuck stuck their feet in each other's crotches in an effort to unlace each other's boots, as the cold was causing their frozen leather boots to swell and press in on their feet, cutting off circulation. But their fingers went numb the moment they touched the laces. Frostbite was now almost guaranteed.

Wrote Connor, "We knew that if we didn't get those boots undone we were going to lose our toes. We worked at it maybe half an hour, but finally we just said, 'Screw it, Let 'em freeze.' That's pretty remarkable. We were not people of low willpower, and to just sit there and say, 'Well, I guess I'm going to give up my toes because I'm too tired to get my boots off,' is hard to imagine."

The altitude and its lack of oxygen, the cold and their state of fatigue, conspired to create a potentially fatal state of apathy in them all. Yet thoughts of rappelling down the south face were, in their assessment, out of the question. They felt that to try to head down with only loose rock and snow to anchor the ropes to would be suicide. The way out of this mess was to climb up to the top and descend the other side. So they waited for the next twelve hours, huddled on the ledge, a knot of arms and legs clinging to the edges of the sleeping bags they had blanketed themselves with to fend off the wind.

By the sixth day they were able to move. "The thing that really startles me is how we were able to get up and climb," said Connor. "I think you realize you have no choice. You can't stop there and you can't go down. In a way it's even kind of a mental relief for everything to be immaterial but one goal. You have to climb, and you have to do it yourself. You have to get to the top, and you have to keep from falling."

Connor had endured the wind a little better than Chuck or Guy, so he took the lead up the ridge in front of them for the next few pitches. Of this pitch Connor wrote, "I led a very steep snow covered rock pitch that seemed like climbing styrofoam peanuts on a steep glass wall."

Any fall would have been deadly, as the protection and belays they rigged along the way would have ripped out under any weight. When his "boys came up looking a bit weary" he continued leading the ridge, which became narrow as a knife edge.

They made a sixth bivouac below a rock outcrop at around 21,500 feet. This one was much more comfortable than the previous night. They cooked a large meal and drank two quarts of liquid each as they settled down in their bags. They discussed the likelihood of frostbite damage to their toes. "When numbness is a constant companion as it was for the entire day, we knew there was tissue damage. In our precarious position, we couldn't afford to attempt treatment or therapy. We had to get over and off this mountain as quickly as possible and worry about the damage when we were safely off the mountain." Connor cautioned both Guy and Chuck not to remove their boots under any circumstances. They could loosen the laces for circulation, but if they removed their boots, their feet would swell hugely, dooming their escape from the peak.

The next morning Connor continued leading his team forward till they reached the end of the hard climbing and were on a huge, almost flat plateau that exited the south face and joined the top of the Polish route. The remainder of the climb was a hike, and so they decided to discard their ropes to save weight. For four hours they trudged over ridges, expecting the summit to appear, but another ridge always awaited them over each rise. Their energy and physical state were by now critical. By then, they knew they had frostbite on their toes and fingers. Around five P.M. they encountered what appeared to be the final obstacle to the summit—a very steep ridge of broken rock. Climbing it would be like walking a tightrope. With thousands of feet of exposure dropping off to either side, to fall would be to die.

They lingered here in a quandary, because night was coming on and El Viento Blanco was building up again. They were concerned about the ridge not leading directly to the summit and getting stranded in an even more exposed position for the night. The wind was already strong enough to knock them off their feet and they had to hold on to rocks to keep from being blown off the ridge. Chuck was now staggering, increasingly helpless with each hour. Judging Chuck to be nearly broken down from exhaustion, Connor told Guy, "We can't take him over right now," so they crouched together in a huddle and bivouacked again, for a seventh night, at around 22,500 feet.

"We bivied in the boulders," wrote Connor, "and spent a very unpleasant night as El Viento Blanco visited us again. The ridge above this platform looked even more exposed and we knew the summit would be very exposed with little snow to dig into."

It was another night in which they could not light the stove and melt water or cook. By morning the wind was still howling. Again they had to wait. Connor still was holding his own against the elements, and he told the boys to wait while he set off down the mountain a short way to look for a more sheltered spot. His six-two, 180-pound body and his mental maturity seemed to sustain him. He found a spot and waved them down, but Chuck and Guy stumbled down without taking their packs. Connor went back up and dragged the packs down. There they spent their eighth night on Aconcagua.

Connor had by this time ceased keeping his journal, but he later told a reporter, "The guys had done a magnificent climb . . . Nobody should be up there for nearly two days after they've done a six-day, 10,000-foot face and gone through what we went through. Nobody should have to put up with that. Nobody should have survived it."

Clear skies and little wind met them on the ninth morning. All three were by then suffering from the altitude and frostbite. "We were thinking strictly of survival at this point," said Connor. "We abandoned all our gear, cut our loads to the bare minimum; just sleeping bags, a bivouac sack and a couple candy bars each. Didn't even carry ice axes."

They were counting on the route being easy, and they knew that on the way down the north side they would find huts and maybe even other climbers. They simply had to keep it together to get over the final hump. Connor claimed the boys were able to function well enough to pack their backpacks and eat and drink the three quarts of water Connor painstakingly melted and poured into their cups. He talked to them about the final section to the top and he instructed them to pace themselves by taking sets of five steps, then breathing deeply, and then taking another set of five steps. He would go ahead to break the trail, telling them to follow.

Connor described this critical moment later in a letter to me: "I told them if we lost visual contact, I would wait a while on the summit, and if I didn't see them there, I would meet them at the first hut on the trail back down. It seemed totally innocent. With the wind in a lull, a full meal in their stomachs, there was not the sense of desperation we had felt the previous day. They understood and acknowledged my instructions with no sign of the erratic response that typifies diminished capacity at altitude. 'Fine,' they said. As we started off, I glanced over at Guy and Chuck and we gave each other a thumbs up as they were helping each other tighten straps and head out." Then Connor headed on. He would never see them again.

Without the gale-force wind the final ridge was not difficult. Connor reached the summit in just over an hour. He realized with frustration that they had sat an entire day at a point just under 300 feet from the top. He waited on top for over an hour but saw no sign of his companions. Once he tried to reverse his tracks to look for them, but exhaustion overtook him and he feared for his own survival: "I took a few steps back down the route and my knees buckled. It was only then I realized the surge of adrenaline that got me up the last few meters had passed and I was dangerously weak from the ordeal of the past week. This was the first time my internal red flags went up. I could see about half the route back to the bivouac and they should have been in sight by now. The summit was a flat exposed plateau about an acre in size. There was a summit marker consisting of some tent poles tied together with wire and some loose tent poles scattered about nearby. I spotted what looked like the descent route to the Berlin Hut, which was visible directly below me. Closer inspection revealed this route to be much more technical than the descriptions we had studied, so I kept looking to the west side of the summit plateau. Here I found the Canoleta, a wide sloping gully that we had read about as being the final feature below the summit from that side. I fashioned a large arrow on the ground from two of the loose aluminum tent poles pointing to the Canoleta in the event they became confused on the summit."

Finally, feeling the wind rise again, he turned and headed down a foot-worn trail through the rubble.

Some twenty years later, Connor described to me the details of his descent alone. He was so tired he was reduced to sliding on his rear and dragging his ice ax over the rocks behind him to make downward progress. It took him three to four hours to reach the hut, which was nothing more than four walls. The roof had blown off years earlier. He collapsed into his sleeping bag and dozed. Three more hours passed. He had expected Chuck and Guy to appear within an hour. Then it got dark. At that point Connor knew the boys would never arrive; another night spent in the open would kill them.

El Viento Blanco blew its hundred-mile-per-hour anger all that night. "I don't think I've ever had a worse night mentally," Connor said later. "I was truly anxious for the first time about something other than technical difficulties. I knew I was dangerously weak and barely able to organize my thoughts about the options available to me. I kept rationalizing they would be along any second. There wasn't a damned thing I could do but sit there and listen to the wind howl. In total exhaustion and despair, I cried myself to sleep fearing the worst for the first time."

Next day—his tenth on Aconcagua—Connor reached a hut and met three Venezuelan climbers. One of them ran down to alert a rescue party, while the others helped Connor to the base of the mountain. But the wind and storm conditions prevented any search for four more days. When rescuers reached the summit, they found no one. At the bivouac where Connor had last seen the boys there was only one ice ax—Guy's. Gear lay strewn about. Guy's boots lay abandoned in the snow. Rescuers noticed that the heels had been sliced open with a knife, apparently to accommodate his painfully bloated feet. That last morning his feet had been so badly swollen that he had put on a pair of tennis shoes that Connor had been carrying in his pack. Connor had hoped to use these tennis shoes for the walk back to base camp. The only other object the rescuers found was a talisman that Guy's mother had given him before the climb.

A few days after this sad incident—on Sunday, January 13—a friend of Kathy's was reading a newspaper in Los Angeles and came across an article that read "Two U.S. Mountain Climbers Found Frozen to Death on Aconcagua." The story named Chuck and Guy as being "presumed

Chuck doing what he loved most. (BOB HILL)

dead," and reported that the army had found the bodies and Connor near the summit. Almost simultaneously, Trish was in a restaurant and read the same story. The headline was erroneous—no bodies had been found. But the news was shocking nonetheless. A flurry of phone calls between members of the families led them to contact the U.S. embassy in Argentina, where some of the details of the incident were confirmed. From the hospital in Mendoza, Connor called Steve Van Meter and asked him to pass on a message to the families saying that it was true that the two men were missing. After Connor returned to the United States, he "spent a tearful couple of hours with Guy Andrews' father at a public park." But he never spoke to Guy's mother or the Bludworths because he was told that they would be "too upset" to visit with him in person.

Those of us who were close to Chuck lived in a confused world for several days in which we believed against all reason that this was a muddle and that Chuck would phone to say he was alive and would be home soon. But gradually it sank in that Chuck was dead. And we learned that during the time of Chuck's darkest hours strange things had happened to some of us. There was Kathy's premonition in the snowbound tent in Yosemite. And while sitting in my room, Tom saw the framed poster of the famous climber Willi Unsoeld suddenly fall off the wall for no reason. "No goal is too high if we climb with care and confidence," were the words inscribed on the poster.

One night I lay in my bed thinking of Chuck, struggling to accept he would never return. I said into the darkness, "Okay, Chuck, if you are dead, come to see me now." Maybe I imagined it, but I felt that his presence entered my room.

Then I was certain he was gone from us forever.

To this day, the bodies of Chuck Bludworth and Guy Andrews have not been found.

I already knew long before Chuck's death that I would never be a mountaineer. I was never drawn to that realm of ice and altitude, nor was my body suited to the cold or for carrying loads that weighed nearly as much as I. Chuck's or anyone's fascination with high-altitude climbing remained mysterious to me. I imagined that climbing with ice axes, crampons, and other sharp devices in cold, oxygen-starved places would create a barrier between the climber and the climb. I loved the touch and feel of the rock, and the intimacy between climber and cliff. That, to me, was beauty.

But even more alien to me was the idea of expeditions. So often, expeditions I have heard about seemed comprised of people who share nothing but an ambition to climb a mountain, to accomplish a "first," or to plant a flag. I did not understand how Chuck could set out on an expedition on which life itself was at stake with people with whom he had barely ever climbed and hardly knew.

Although the experience of losing Chuck affected me deeply, there was no question in my mind that I would continue climbing after he passed away. Our shared passion for climbing and the experiences we lived together will always remain a part of me.

Chapter 6

Yosemite Days

In the early 1980s climbers from all over America and the world congregated in Yosemite Valley. They ensconced themselves there in a seasonal tent village named Camp Four, where many lived like a ragged occupying army, annoying park rangers by eluding camp fees, overstaying their welcome, and comporting themselves like gypsies. In the mornings, we climbers gathered in the now-defunct parking lot beside the lodge and the Four Seasons Restaurant, an eatery we dubbed the Foul Seasons, Foul Regions, or Foul Squeezin's, depending on the state of your digestive system after a meal there. The parking lot had been irreverently renamed the Arcing Plot by some climber as a commentary on the electric vibe emanating from the climbing crowd. This field of blacktop served as our de facto town square where, in between games of Hacky Sack, climbing plans were hatched and the long-haired luminaries of the scene held court. This was our neighborhood and these people created the community that gave me a sense of belonging.

Long before Yosemite Valley became a mecca to climbers, it was a place of inspiration to the Ahwahnee Tribe, who lived there for centuries. In the late 1800s explorers like John Muir wrote of the grandeur of thunderstorms rolling over the valley rim from the High Sierras, and later Ansel Adams communicated the same natural drama through his camera lens. When climbers began showing up in Yosemite in the post–World War II years, they found that the sun-bathed rock was impeccably solid, with cracks and features that made it a joy to dance over. With cliffs of every dimension—from house-sized rocks with short boulder problems of ferocious difficulty to 100-foot cliffs split by perfect cracks to immense walls that may take two weeks to ascend—Yosemite earned its reputation as the one of the very finest places on earth to climb.

Glaciers had gouged this canyon out of Sierra Nevada bedrock eons ago. When the Ice Age was over and the ice caps had melted, a 3,000-foot-deep, five-mile-wide corridor of rocky turrets and buttresses was revealed. In the highest reaches of the valley are the solid granite mountains of Half Dome and Mount Watkins, facing each other with walls so smooth they look as if a knife had slashed through the sky, slicing the timeworn, rounded domes in half. Downstream along the Merced River stand great portals of rock like Washington Column, the spear-pointed Lost Arrow Spire with thundering Yosemite Falls beside it, and the dark-faced tombstone of Sentinel Rock. Farther downstream still, amid grassy meadows and stands of huge sequoias, are other spectacular formations: the Leaning Tower, Middle Cathedral Rock, and the mightiest stone of all, El Capitan, which rises abruptly on the south flank of the valley in a clean, tawny sweep for 3,000 feet. If you take the secular view of existence, then Yosemite is a wonderfully sculpted geologic accident; if you believe in a cosmic master plan, then it is among the Creator's greatest works, a natural wonder of the world.

My visits to Yosemite in my teen years—from ages sixteen to nineteen—were always wedged between going to school and various part-time jobs like teaching gymnastics at Cal State University at Fullerton or flipping burgers in fast-food joints. Yet improving my skills on rock and living in the midst of Yosemite's walls to learn about the adventures of those climbers who had been there before me seemed, to me, as important as anything school had to offer. And with a climbing legend written in every wall, Yosemite was like a library of America's vertical history.

One of the legends that inspired my great respect and admiration for the early pioneers of Yosemite climbing concerned the Lost Arrow Spire, one of the most striking of all Yosemite towers. This 200-foot spire of rock sticks out like a thumb from the main wall from a point 1,200 feet above the ground. The year was 1946, a time when none of the major walls in Yosemite had been climbed, and the man of the moment was a Swiss-born blacksmith and vegetarian named John Salathè.

As is so often the case in climbing, it was a piece of equipment that shaped the destiny of the sport, and in the case of the Lost Arrow Spire, it was a piton. After World War II, the only pitons available were made of soft steel. Though these suited the soft limestone rock of Europe

Chuck relaxing on top of the Lost Arrow Spire while Bob makes his way across the spectacular Tyrolean traverse. (BOB HILL COLLECTION)

where they were manufactured, they were too malleable to use on hard Yosemite granite. Salathè learned this the hard way, while trying to be the first climber to reach the pointy tip of the Lost Arrow. On that attempt his soft pitons bent and deformed when he hammered them into cracks, and he'd ended up with a mangled, unusable pile of metal. Even though he was close to the top he had no choice but to retreat, because he was dependent on hanging directly from each piton. This was the accepted tactic back then: rather than free climb steep rock, one hammered in a ladder of pitons, a method we still call "aid climbing."

Bent pitons didn't deter Salathè. Turning to his blacksmith skills, he fired up his forge at home and took to the axle of a salvaged Model-A Ford, heating up slivers he'd cut from it until they glowed white-hot, and pounding them into a new type of piton. Made of carbon steel, his new designs were stronger and more durable than the old iron pitons, and they were better shaped to fit the cracks of Yosemite. They even resembled the shape of the Lost Arrow Spire, and climbers quickly began referring to them as exactly that—Lost Arrows. To help his ascent of the Lost Arrow, Salathè also fashioned a claw-shaped device that resembled a grappling hook, which he draped over the edges of flakes on the rock face and hung from. Today, climbers on El Cap carry such devices—called skyhooks—on most major big-wall aid routes. Salathè also took his bolt drills and tempered them with heat so the hard Yosemite rock would not blunt them. Finally, he refined the rope tactics he used, devising a system that is similar to that used today. Salathè caught my attention not only because of these technical breakthroughs, but also for his mental outlook: he had the faith in himself to try things no one had tried before.

John Salathè, teamed up with Anton Nelson, had already made the first ascent of the southwest face of Half Dome, in a twenty-four-hour push. That was probably the hardest climb in America at the time, but when the pair turned to the Lost Arrow Spire and began climbing a deep fissure splitting the wall behind the spire, they entered for the first time an even harder realm—the realm of true "big-wall climbing," ascents of huge cliffs that may take several days and nights to climb. Knowing their route would take longer than Half Dome, and that they would not be able to carry enough water for their multiday ascent, they conditioned themselves on other climbs to drink sparingly. Several weeks of this camellike training prepared them for a thirsty five-day climb of the Lost Arrow Chimney. Salathè's last stroke of genius came in July 1950, when he and Allen Steck—who was still making appearances in Camp Four when I was in Yosemite—climbed the north face of Sentinel Rock over four and a half days. Climbers still regard that route as a strenuous challenge.

Thirty years later, when my Yosemite career began, the gear, standards, and mental attitudes about climbing had come a long way. Instead of having only steel pitons, we also had nuts and cams that gently and easily slotted into cracks. We had better climbing shoes, stronger ropes, and more efficient devices to fulfill nearly every need on a wall. In addition, our more athletic style of training and the balletlike free climbing movements we had perfected allowed us to dance on our fingers and toes over many sections of rock that Salathè would have aid-climbed. Yet though we were climbing harder routes, I doubt we were climbing with more boldness or vision than Salathè, for nothing can compare with the demands of confronting the unknown.

In the summer of 1979 I stood in the Arcing Plot racking up a pile of climbing gear for an ascent of that most famous of all Yosemite routes, the Nose of El Capitan. The route, established in 1958, had been the first line up El Capitan. Days before the first climbers began work on the Nose, the steep north face of Half Dome had fallen to Royal Robbins, Jerry Gallwas, and Mike Sherrick. El Cap, towering at the opposite end of the valley from Half Dome, was the next frontier to explore. Nothing like it had ever been climbed before. The time, energy, and persistence required to do the first ascent of such a huge wall of rock was an adventure on a par with the race to the South Pole.

The biggest, steepest, most technical rock climb ever attempted caught the public eye more than any climb in America before it. Several climbers worked on the Nose, going up and down on fixed ropes on several attempts spread between July 4, 1957, and November 12, 1958. The sight of the climbers dangling on the wall had caused traffic jams in the valley below, and at one point a ranger had stood in the meadow shouting to a climber through a bullhorn, "Get your ass down from there!" The Park Service didn't warm to the vertical shenanigans going on above them and they initially banned the climb, but finally they relented, letting the climbers continue to push the route higher as long as they agreed to climb during the off-season in Yosemite—after Labor Day and before Memorial Day. These restrictions, the still-primitive gear, and the slow-moving nature of aid climbing almost the entire route contributed to the huge number of climbing days spent on the wall: forty-five, spread over a period of nearly eighteen months.

The mastermind of the Nose's first ascent, and the only man part of it from beginning to end during those intensive months, was a climbing visionary named Warren Harding. Harding later wrote a strange book called *Downward Bound* in which he chronicled in comic form the Yosemite scene of the 1960s, poking fun at the vanities and conceits of every climber, including himself, whom he painted as a wine-swilling maverick. In the book he constantly referred to himself by his nickname, Batso, which was derived from his batty outlook on life, his bat-like habit of living on cliffs, and also a collection of angular facial features and a slicked-back, vampiresque hairline. Wine jug in hand, an older, more stoop-shouldered version of Harding strolled through Camp Four occasionally while I was camping there. He still climbed, but he seemed to avoid the Arcing Plot with its younger, more hippie-looking crowd. Just as I would come to feel some day in the future, Harding felt that his heyday in Yosemite had passed, but he still loved the place and couldn't get it out of his system.

My partners on the Nose were to be two Joshua Tree regulars, Mari Gingery and Dean Fidelman. By this stage, I had already climbed a few big-wall routes like the Regular and Direct routes on Half Dome, the south face of Mount Watkins, and other one-day wall routes like the Rostrum and Sentinel Rock. But I had done these climbs with people who had experience superior to mine, and I had to some extent relied on their know-how to get us up. On the Nose, the partnership would be more equally aligned. The Nose would be steeper and longer than anything I had previously climbed, and it involved a lot of aid climbing, something at which none of us was very experienced. For each of us, the Nose was to be a great learning opportunity.

Dean, a member of the J-Tree scene, felt like family, so when he expressed a desire to come along on the Nose, I figured his good humor and endless supply of wisecracks would come in handy. Mari, a soft-spoken research biologist specializing in electron microscopy in LA, felt like family too. She had become a regular partner of mine over many weekend jaunts to the southern California cliffs. On those weekends we had often been the only women in a sea of coarse-talking, hard-cranking men. We had found a sisterhood in figuring out our own methods of getting up sections of routes the guys simply muscled through. Since I was always the smallest person around, I had to use the strength and flexibility I had developed through gymnastics to get past sections where taller people could reach a hold. Born to a German-American father and a Japanese mother, raven-haired Mari has a slight build too, though she is several inches taller than me. Gifted with a balletlike climbing style, she was able to use sensitivity and technique to pass difficult sections. We shared a love of free climbing, and a big part of our devotion came from the joy of figuring out our own unique choreography of movement using the natural features of the rock.

On some of those weekends at Joshua Tree, I remember how Mari and I would lose track of time, like children playing, as we roamed the desert from one boulder to another, climbing until our skin burned from the sharp rock and we couldn't hang onto the holds any longer. At such times we'd examine our chalk-white hands with their callused skin and frayed nails and cuticles, and we'd joke about needing a manicure.

Loitering around us in the Arcing Plot that day, as we sorted gear and packed our haulbags with enough food and water for three days on the Nose, were several men and, in far lesser numbers, the women who comprised the hard core of the Yosemite climbing scene. Shirts off to soak up the morning sun, the men had bodies honed from a thousand strenuous rock climbs, and the sunlight beaming in over the north rim of the valley highlighted the ridges and troughs of their muscles. As paunchy middle-aged tourists strolled by on their way to breakfast or to sightseeing tours, they cast openmouthed glances at this living statuary of enviably fit young people. "They must be the climbers," tourists could be heard whispering.

Most of the usual Joshua Tree crowd had moved into Yosemite that summer. Largo, Yabo, Mike Lechlinski, Bachar, and others were standing in clusters around the van-choked parking lot, talking to Yosemite habitués like Jim Bridwell, Ron Kauk, Dale Bard, Mark Chapman,

The Joshua Tree gang. Left to right—back row: Yabo, Mari Gingery, Mike Lechlinski, Randy Vogal; middle row: Dave Evans, Maria Cranor, Largo, Charles Cole, Dean Fidelman, Jim Angione, Craig Fry; front: Brian Rennie. (BRIAN RENNIE)

Werner Braun, and Kevin Worrall. Collectively, this group represented some of the top American climbers of the day. Occasionally they offered advice on what we should take, or loaned us an item of gear we were lacking. "Racking up" is part of the ritual for a big-wall climb, and neatly laying out on the ground one's arsenal of gear and supplies is like arraying the ranks of one's army before charging into the foe. For the Nose we had assembled an array of hexentrics and stoppers for sticking in cracks; a few pitons; fifty carabiners clipped into a long, silvery chain; jumars and aid slings for ascending the rope; three hefty leading and hauling ropes; a pulley to make it easier to drag the haulbag up the wall; six gallon jugs of water; a stuff sack crammed with bagels, canned tuna, candy bars, and dried fruit; sleeping bags and foam pads.

While we sorted through this mounting pile, a distorting pair of car speakers blared a Jimi Hendrix riff over the distant roar of Yosemite

Falls. This provided dramatic mood music to a tale that Jim Bridwell, a.k.a. the Bird or the Admiral, was telling, about a death-defying aid pitch he had led on a new route that he and Kim Schmitz had recently completed on Half Dome. The route was called Zenith, and it climbed a patch of granite so steep that raindrops had never touched the 2,000-foot face. The pitch had an airy name: the Space Flake.

Bridwell was the undisputed leader of the climbing scene in Yosemite Valley at this time, and when he spoke, people listened. Tall, dusty-haired, leather-faced, muscle-bound, and sporting a droopy and seditious-looking Che Guevara mustache, he had, at age thirty-six, been climbing longer than some of us had been alive. He had also mastered many of the hardest, tallest routes in Yosemite. As John Long once jokingly remarked, Bridwell was old enough "to have known the Unknown Soldier and who shot him. In a manner, a rope ran from him back to the very beginnings of the sport." Moreover, he was also highly supportive of my climbing goals almost from the moment I met him.

"We are fifteen hundred feet off the deck and the wall overhangs thirty degrees beyond the vertical," Bridwell was saying of his climb up Zenith. "We get to this flake. It looks like a guillotine blade, only it's a hundred feet long, and it hangs over our heads like a death sentence. Schmitz says, 'No way, this thing is too dangerous, one tap of the hammer and it'll cleave us off the wall.' So we sit there for a long time, looking at it before I get the balls to start up."

Bridwell holds the young crowd's attention as he relates his tale. He describes with a mechanic's knack for technical detail the tricky ways he made each piece of his gear wedge into the gaping mouth of the flake. Bridwell's description is so vivid I can almost hear the flake vibrate like a gong as he drives pitons behind it with his hammer. He makes us feel that for every piece of gear he placed in that hundred heart-stopping feet there was an exact number of taps of the hammer to make it stick. One tap too few and the piece would rip out when he was hanging from it, creating a zipperlike fall that would send him careening like a wrecking ball into Schmitz. One tap too many and the tension of the flake would be broken, and hundreds of tons of razor-edged flake would snap off into Bridwell's lap, slicing off his legs, cutting the rope, and wiping Schmitz off the wall with him. Bridwell's ability to know precisely how many hammer blows to make and not kill himself seemed less guesswork and more testimony to his reputation as being a Zen master of big-wall climbing.

Jim Bridwell was not the only climber doing new routes in Yosemite back then, but for three decades beginning in the mid-1960s (culminating with his heyday of new climbs in the late 1970s), he was the king of Yosemite climbing. Bridwell's devotion to climbing typified a growing attitude of many climbers at the time: rather than follow the path of career, job, and secure future, he realized that the only way to climb well was to devote all one's time to the activity. Odd jobs and infrequent work sufficed to keep him going in between his demanding climbs. But he reaped great rewards from his adventures.

Jim had been born in 1944 in San Antonio, Texas. His father was a war hero and officer in the Army Air Corps, so he had moved about from one air base to another in classic army-brat style. As a teenager he displayed a talent for delivering fastballs for his high school baseball team, but another family move pulled him away from organized sports. The Bridwells moved to San Mateo, California, where Jim took up more solitary activities like hiking in the redwoods and falconry. In fact, his interest in visiting steep places was sparked by his curiosity to examine the nests of birds of prey. A visit to Yosemite sealed his fate as a climber, and he left school at age nineteen and headed to the valley. Quite quickly, Bridwell teamed up with an intense, energetic man some considered another demigod of Yosemite climbing, Frank Sacherer.

Bridwell's natural athleticism translated well into the brawny nature of 1960s free climbing that Sacherer espoused. These were the early days of the free climbing revolution, when climbers were just starting to realize the beauty of free climbing up the rock unaided by equipment. Yet it was still long before the invention of the easy-to-place spring-loaded camming devices that we take for granted today, let alone the ultrastrong bolts of millennium-era sport climbing. Pitons were the main form of protection and consequently most routes followed cracks. This meant that the climber led with a twenty-pound rack of steel pitons slung around his neck, and a hammer in a holster at his waist. The climber would lead up a few feet, then hang one-armed from a likely hold, fiddle a piton off one of the carabiners that stored it, slot the piton into the crack, then pound it in with the hammer. It was a strenuous, ungainly technique, more like being a steelworker than a climber. It also forced the lead climber to climb with daring. Because it was so strenuous to dangle one-handed to hammer in a piton, the leader frequently "ran it out" for long distances before finding a spot to hammer a piton in for protection. It was dangerous, but there was no other way; the equipment that was available governed the method. This need to accept risk in order to free climb a route created a culture of climbing that embraced and admired boldness. This tactic also gave birth to some ground rules of climbing that would last for many years before they were rethought.

The main rules were as follows:

Rule One: All climbs started on the ground. If you inspected a route from above by rappelling down a fixed rope, or if you placed protection on the route from above by this method, you had failed on the climb and you had cheated.

Rule Two: If you fell while leading, you had to immediately lower back down to the ground and start again. If you hung from any protection along the route, you had also failed and cheated.

These rules became commandments for us during the 1970s and 1980s, and when some climbers began to deviate from these tactics in later years, there were great controversies, fiery letters to the editors of many magazines, and even fistfights. Eventually, though, by the late 1980s, these philosophies would be almost entirely tossed out of the rule book of climbing. Not only did the equipment evolve, but also the vision and methods of free climbing changed, and these rules became virtually obsolete. The emphasis veered away from the mountaineering heritage of climbing in which risk and danger were considered integral to the experience, and toward making routes with rappel-placed bolts on which new levels of difficulty could be safely explored. But when I started climbing, these rules were law.

Embracing the doctrine of boldness, Sacherer and his protégé Bridwell climbed many famous routes together: Ahab (5.10), Crack of Doom (5.10d), and the first free ascent of a two-day route called the North Buttress of Middle Cathedral Rock (5.10a) were all on the tick-lists of Yosemite aspirants when I first arrived. When I met Bridwell, he was, in the manner of a tribal elder, passing on to us youngsters the bold lessons he had gleaned from Sacherer. Those lessons, passed on like a religion, included throwing oneself at routes with abandon, stepping over the line of commitment to give one's all, physically and mentally, even if it sometimes meant getting into dangerous situations. Sacherer left Yosemite in 1966 to work in Europe as a physicist. In the late 1970s he was climbing in the French Alps, on an ice route called the Shroud on the Grandes Jorasses, when lightning struck and killed him. Said Bridwell of his mentor's place in climbing history, "He had free climbed routes that the best climbers of the day said couldn't be done free. He had climbed routes in a day they said couldn't be done in a day. In the 1960s Sacherer did more to advance free climbing as we know it today than any other single person."

After Sacherer, Bridwell became the leader of the pack, surrounding

Jumaring up the first pitch of the Nose in 1979. (JESSICA PERRIN-LARRABEE)

himself like a Roman general with talented young warrior-climbers with whom he could team up to pluck off the scores of new routes that awaited the bold. The soaring hand-jamming cracks of Outer Limits (5.10c) and New Dimensions (5.11a) were some of his best free climbs of the early 1970s, and they taught me much about the art of climbing steep cracks. But no lessons were more keenly felt than those I learned on my first time up the Nose of El Capitan.

Vertigo, fear of heights, exposure—call it what you will, but the sense of adrenaline, or excitement, that we feel when standing on the edge of a huge cliff is part of our internal mechanism. Someday, I suspect, geneticists will unravel a part of our DNA to find a gene that governs the way we each react to heights, and parents will be able to test their children to determine whether they'll be BASE jumpers who leap off cliffs, or people who shiver with horror when gazing over a lookout. As Mari, Dean, and I got higher and higher on the airy, soaring Nose that first day of climbing, it became apparent which of us had the fear-of-heights gene and which of us didn't.

I could tell that something was wrong with Dean when his sense of humor vanished on the first day. His attitude suddenly became serious when he had to lead a pitch that required him to perform a maneuver called a pendulum. By that time we were 500 feet off the ground, high enough that we could look straight down onto the tips of the towering pines of Yosemite Valley. From our vantage point they resembled so many pencils jammed into the earth. We had begun the climb planning to share the leads, meaning that each person would lead every third pitch. But after Dean finished his pitch, he turned pale, jittery, and serious. He had just gotten through hanging at the end of the rope and running back and forth across the wall, swinging like a clock pendulum, until he gained enough momentum to dive at a crack 40 feet to his right. It was a rough-and-tumble maneuver, certain to terrify anyone prone to a fear of heights.

"I think I'll just hand over the leading to you girls," he said when I ascended the rope and hung next to him on a ledgeless patch of the wall.

"What? Don't you want to lead the next bit? It's a great-looking pitch," Mari said.

"It's okay, you can take it."

"No, really, go for it Dean, you'll have fun."

"No way, I don't want to lead anymore."

"Oh, go on, take the rack and—"

"Goddammit, I said no. I'm staying here. I'll jumar up behind you," he snapped back with a characteristic "Bullwinkle crinkle" in his brow.

Mari and I exchanged a look as if to say, *Okay, we'll take over the lead.* We all realized that at this point the only way down for Dean was up—behind us. For the rest of the day Dean hugged close to the rock as he ascended the ropes in our wake. I could tell from his rapid, nervy breathing and the beads of sweat pearling on his brow that he was not comfortable at this height. Perhaps the way Mari and I reveled in the verticality of El Cap—leaning back into the air in our harnesses, standing with our toes on the edge of ledges and peering down into the void—made him even more nervous. Years later, when I found myself feeling uneasy on a steep snowfield in the mountains of Kyrgyzstan I could relate to what Dean must have felt. Snow, I discovered, is a medium of the steep with which I have no affinity other than for skiing or snowboarding.

The Nose route goes right up the center of El Capitan, following a prominent prow that juts forward—just like a beak. Splitting this protrusion of rock is a crack system that is, by a quirk of geology, just the right size for a human to securely jam his or her fingers, hands, or body into. With only occasional blank spots, this 3,000-foot fissure forms a vertical highway to the summit of El Capitan.

Alternating leads, Mari and I moved steadily up, clipping into old pitons, and placing our own jangling cord-threaded nuts and hexagons into the crack as well. Sometimes we free climbed, up to 5.10 in difficulty, and sometimes we hung our bodies from the gear and aid climbed. Meanwhile, Dean climbed up behind us, ascending the ropes on his jumars, which are clamps with a handgrip; a jumar slides up a rope, but it locks on to the rope when one pulls down on it. Jumars are a Swiss invention, and they have had such an impact on climbing that the verb "jumar" has become part of the climbing lexicon.

About 700 feet up we came to a 500-foot-long section of unusually wide crack called the Stovelegs. The story of the way the first ascent team climbed this section in 1958 is another of those moments in climbing where necessity was the mother of invention. The question of how Harding and his crew would get themselves up the Stovelegs had been debated around Camp Four for weeks, as no one had ever invented protection to climb such a wide crack before. Although Salathè was beating out his custom-made Lost Arrows on his anvil as fast as climbers could hammer them into cracks, no one was making wide pitons, so therefore there was no equipment available for anyone to climb a feature like the Stovelegs. But when Harding's friend Frank Tarver found an old wood-burning stove while scavenging through the Berkeley city dump, he realized that the prettily enameled angle-iron legs of the stove could provide the solution to this section of the climb. Armed with the four heavy nine-inch-long legs, Harding reached the Stovelegs crack on July 8, 1957. Hammering the legs into the crack and clipping their rope around them for protection, the team leapfrogged them upward for several hundred feet to get to a point just below a prominent, flat-topped landmark now known as Dolt Tower. At that point, with their stove legs beaten and bent, and the Park Service shouting at them to descend, they retreated to the valley floor.

In more recent years climbers had found that it was no great problem to free climb the Stovelegs, and Mari and I inserted our hands into the crack and squeezed our fists into balls, using a special technique called jamming. Each hand jam was almost as secure as gripping the rung of a ladder. We moved up in this fashion, with our feet walking up the crack in a ladderlike lockstep. This went on for four pitches. The crack ended at Dolt Tower, named after Bill Feurer, a.k.a. Dolt, one of Harding's partners.

On this ledge, a few historical moments played out during the first ascent. While Wally Reed was prusiking up the team's fixed ropes, using a technique to ascend that preceded the invention of the jumar, he noticed that the ropes were beginning to show signs of wear. The next thing he knew, he found himself plummeting earthward. The rope had abraded through and he was lucky enough to land on the ledge a short distance below. But perhaps one of the least effective experiments in gear technology was the Dolt Cart. Feurer was an aeronautical engineer, and he came up with an idea for Harding and the rest of them to more easily haul the huge weight of gear, food, and water up the wall for their protracted siege of the Nose. He bolted to the cliff a large steel frame on which was mounted a big pulley—the Dolt Winch. A rope went through this and down to the ground, where it was attached to the most insane-looking bit of climbing gear ever created: the Dolt Cart. This was a cart replete with inflatable bicycle tires onto which the team would lash a fifty-pound haulbag. Harding called the Dolt Cart "a grand sight" as it rolled slowly up the wall on its 1,200-foot journey to Dolt Tower, but the contraption tipped over frequently and got stuck under protrusions of rock. Besides, it took four men to operate the winch and cart. Eventually, after the climbers had wasted several days with this device, it broke down entirely and they resumed the bruising task of dragging haulbags up the slabby wall using pure muscle power. As for us, we hauled our sixty-pound haulbag up each pitch using a small pulley, sweating and grunting under the sun and labor.

Our first bivouac on the Nose was spent on the spacious ledge of El Cap Tower. We laid out our ensolite pads on the flat but hard surface, then snuggled into our sleeping bags. We slept still wearing our harnesses, the rope tying us to the bolt anchors in the wall above the ledge—just in case someone rolled overboard or went sleepwalking. Once we were inside our bags, water jugs and the food sack were pulled from the haulbag and we began devouring our dinner. As Sierra alpenglow saturated the valley in hues of pink, an aerial animal show above our heads changed shifts. The swallows that had been swooping and chattering all day flew at breakneck velocity at the rock face, broke their speed at the last second, and disappeared into the cracks where they nested. Taking their place came the bats, which emerged from dark recesses and entered the night air to hunt for insects.

Tucked into his sleeping bag and positioned as far from the cliff edge as possible, Dean rediscovered his sense of humor. He opened a can with a Swiss army knife and passed it to Mari with the aplomb of a waiter in a ritzy restaurant.

"Madam, would care for some fruit cocktail?" he asked, and he catered to us the rest of the night, passing cookies and chunks of pemmican bar, and passing the water jug as if it were a bottle of fine wine.

The next day we rose early. As the sun brightened the valley, I saw a haze of smog lingering at car level. Above us, on a wildly steep patch of El Cap slightly to our east, a golden light kissed the wall. This was the final section of another of Harding's famous routes, the Dawn

Wall, also called the Wall of Early Morning Light. On this climb, completed in 1970, Harding and Dean Caldwell had spent twenty-seven days climbing and hanging in hammocklike "bat tents," to make the first ascent. This was nearly twice as long as anyone had ever spent continuously living on a wall. The ascent was, in the parlance of climbing, an "epic." The pair had set out on this highly technical aid climb with five haulbags weighing a total of three hundred pounds, plus eighty pounds of hardware (mostly pitons), twelve gallons of water, and several jugs of Christian Brothers wine. (The winery eventually used an image of Harding on the wall, tippling a glass of their finest, in an ad campaign.)

The climbers moved slowly, finding that they had to laboriously drill bolts and rivets to get through huge blank sections. They struck a hand-held drill handle with the hammer, every bolt hole requiring several hundred blows to drill out. A four-day rainstorm drenched the pair when they were about one-third of the way up, and their cocoonlike bat tents filled with rainwater. When the storm cleared, it was the fifteenth day of an intended fifteen-day climb. But they didn't give up, rationing food and water instead. They'd share half a can of fruit for breakfast

The visionary Warren Harding in 1968. (GALEN ROWELL)

and half a can of sardines for dinner. After twenty-three days the Park Service mounted a rescue and an Air Force helicopter circled in front of them, while a climber was lowered from the rim on a rope. "We attacked the rescuer . . . with a torrent of profanity and drove him back up the wall," wrote Harding in his book. They would not be rescued, and when they pulled over the top on November 19, they were greeted by more than a hundred reporters and observers who had become intrigued at this determined pair.

On the Nose, we had to climb ten pitches from El Cap Tower to reach our next bivouac ledge, a spot known as Camp Five. With Dean now figuratively "in the haulbag," all leading fell to Mari and me. Getting to Camp Five involved climbing up Boot Flake, a wafer of rock that seems to float on the wall and which will surely fall off one day soon—soon being, in geologic terms, sometime between next week and ten thousand years. From the top of Boot Flake, we had to make a giant pendulum called the King Swing, across a large blank face to another crack system 35 feet over to our left. Five pitches after Boot Flake, we stood below the Great Roof. This feature loomed over our heads like a mounting tidal wave. At the time, no climber in the world imagined that such a feature could be free climbed. Fifteen years later climbers would recant that belief but would find the Great Roof to be one of the hardest sections to free climb on the entire route.

"There are still two pitches before our bivy, and the sun is pretty low," I shouted to Mari, urging her to hurry through the aid climbing that lay ahead of her.

"Yeah, I know," she said, moving methodically from piece to piece. Even on aid climbing—something I consider ungainly and only a necessary evil when free climbing methods fail—Mari moved with precision and grace.

Forty minutes after she started the Great Roof pitch, she was nearing the belay, 120 feet above me. Mari shouted down that to speed our progress I should jumar up the rope she had just led on, "cleaning the pitch," or, in layman's terms, removing the gear she had placed. This would leave Dean to jumar up on our other rope, which would be secured to the belay at the end of the Great Roof. This rope hung out away from the rock and about 40 feet to the side. Though it was completely safe to clip one's jumars onto it and swing out, the idea of dangling around, spinning slowly and dizzyingly above the valley floor while trying to ascend, caused Dean's eyes to boggle.

"I prefer following the pitch rather than jumaring out in space," he said to me flatly.

"No, it'll take too long for you to clean this pitch. Just swing out. It's totally safe."

"No, Lynnie, it's too dangerous," he said urgently. "The rope could get cut up there if I swing out. Remember what happened to Chris Robbins?" he protested, referring to a young climber who, not long before, had been jumaring a dangling rope on an El Cap route called the Tangerine Trip and had fallen to his death when his rope had been severed by rubbing against a sharp edge. But Mari had been careful to check that no such hazard existed in Dean's case.

He carped at me to trade places—for me to jumar the dangling rope while he cleaned Mari's pitch. If night hadn't been approaching, I would have consented, but in my own anxiety to get up to our bivy ledge before dark, my patience was wearing thin. I replied sternly, "We can't afford to wait an extra hour for you to clean this pitch. We don't even have enough daylight left to reach Camp Five."

He moaned, muttered, then sat back and awaited his fate.

"Ready to haul," Mari shouted from the end of the pitch, and I sent the haulbag out into space. Then it was time to send Dean on his way.

"I hate this," he said.

"It will be fine," I tried to reassure him. "Here, I'll hold the end of the rope and slowly lower you out. That way you won't swing so much." I felt bad. Dean looked like a scared cat.

I lowered him out using what slack remained in the rope that he hung from. His unease at leaving the security of the belay ledge showed immediately as he displayed a textbook case of fear of heights. His feet pedaled in the air, and his eyes grew wide and white-rimmed. Then the end of the rope came tight in my hands. At that point I had to let go of it, letting Dean swing violently outward in a great arc that would be more exciting than an E ticket ride at Disneyland.

"No, Lynn, wait . . ." Dean pleaded when he saw the last few inches of rope in my hand. Below him was a drop of 2,000 feet to the toe of El Capitan.

"Sorry, Dean, there's no more rope. I gotta let go."

Just before I let Dean swing out into space, he looked me straight in the eye and said earnestly, "Tell Jessica I love her." Jessica was his girl-friend. Half scared out of his wits, half having the time of his life and looking for a quip to make us laugh, Dean would later repeat this melo-dramatic phrase on a daily basis.

When the rope left my fingers, Dean flew out into the air, screamed, grasped desperately at his jumars, and started to sprint up the rope like a man running from a tiger. I looked up at Mari, 120 feet above me, and we both burst out laughing.

I set about sliding my own jumars up the rope, pausing at the tiny stoppers Mari had placed, giving each one an upward tug till it popped out. All the way up the Great Roof pitch I found myself instinctually feeling the narrow crack with my fingers, trying to imagine what it would be like to free climb through this remarkable piece of natural architecture. Climbers like John Bachar and Ron Kauk had been try-ing to free climb different sections of the Nose in recent years, but everyone was unanimous that the Great Roof would always remain an aid pitch.

"Think it'll ever go free?" Mari asked me when I reached her.

"I don't know," I replied. "The crack is so thin I can hardly get my fingertips into it and the face is as smooth as a mirror." It was my lead next and I quickly began climbing up a golden-colored sliver of rock that looked as if it had been slapped to the wall. This was pitch num-ber twenty-three, the Pancake Flake.

By the time I was ready to lead toward Camp Five, it was pitch-dark. Being novices at the big-wall climbing game none of us even possessed a headlamp. What little moon there was that night hovered behind El Capitan, so the blackness was nearly total.

"Now what?" Dean asked.

"Well, we can't stay here. We'd be standing up all night; we'd never sleep," Mari replied.

"Dean, hand over your cigarette lighter. Maybe I can see the crack well enough with that," I said.

"Whatever you do, don't drop it. If I have to go through this without my smokes, I'll be an even bigger nervous wreck than I am now, believe me."

Dean's deadpan kibitzing got us laughing again. He handed me a Bic lighter. I flicked it on. The flame illuminated a circle of about two feet in front of me, but after a few seconds it got so hot I had to shut it off.

"Better than nothing," I said.

"Don't use up all the butane; it's my only lighter," Dean cautioned as I set off up the pitch.

The pitch that leads to Camp Five is rated 5.11, but most ascents aid climb the entire pitch. At that point in my climbing career, that was nearly as hard as anything I had ever led. Every couple of feet I would pause to light the path with Dean's Bic. The yellow glow would reveal a flash of information—the size of the crack in front of me, a foothold to the right—then I'd let the flame flicker out. I would grope up in the dark a few feet until I got into unknown ground again, then I'd pause again to light up another patch of rock. The crack opened into a V-shaped flare that swallowed my body. I shuffled and groveled. The process became hypnotic. It was neither pleasant nor unpleasant, calming nor terrifying, fun nor drudgery. It was just necessary, and I was simply there, like a bug on the wall, moving inexorably up out of instinct and need. My sense of time evaporated.

When I reached the welcome ledge of Camp Five, it was nearly midnight. I had been climbing by Braille for an hour and a half. As I methodically set up a belay anchor on the ledge, anchored the ropes for Mari and Dean to jumar up, then hauled the bag to the ledge, I had time to think about the altered mental state I had attained during my nocturnal climb. I began to truly see the meaning behind big-wall climbing. The wall was like some living entity that was testing our mettle by throwing up new challenges, new unknowns, that we had to overcome. This was the essence of what guys like Harding and Bridwell were talking about when they described some crazy stunt they were forced to perform during a climb. Because up here there was no turning back and no room for panic. Dealing with a space flake that was about to break off the wall and squash you, or making it through a pitch in the inky dark, were all parts of a journey of self-discovery and self-reliance.

I winched the haulbag onto the ledge just as my partners arrived. As we began securing ourselves into the anchor and trying to lay our sleeping bags out on the ledge to get some sleep, we crisscrossed the ropes into a rat's nest of a tangle. A few bites of food, a gulp of water, and I closed my eyes and entered a deep sleep.

When I woke next morning, I found myself cramped into a back-bending position, on the end of a ledge that was just wide enough for two people. Only my upper body lay on the rocky shelf we were sprawled on; my legs were draped over the edge of the cliff, resting on top of the haulbag. My head felt foggy from too little sleep and too much work. My hands immediately began throbbing; they were swollen and chafed from being stuffed into cracks, and blackened with metal oxides from gripping our carabiners. Worst of all, my tongue felt glued to the roof of my mouth. All I could think about was satiating my thirst.

I leaned over to unclip the water bottle hanging from the anchor, and in doing so I shifted my feet. Out of the corner of my eye I watched my feet kick the food bag out of the top of the haulbag. It was the only item not clipped in to the tangle of gear, ropes, and carabiners that hung all around us. Despair is the only word I know to describe my feeling as all of our food bounced down the wall and into the forest 2,000 feet below.

"What was that, did something just fall off the ledge?" Dean asked groggily.

How was I going to tell a hungry man that the last cans of fruit cocktail and bagels he had been dreaming about were now hurtling toward the scavenging squirrels and blue jays that roam the base of El Cap?

"Oops," was all I could say.

"What now?"

"Well, I'm sorry, but I just dropped the food."

"Perfect," said Dean as he lit his morning cigarette. "I couldn't have fucked up better myself."

At this, we started laughing. It was true. So many things had gone wrong on this climb that this was, as the French say, the coup de grâce—the final blow. There was nothing to do but pack up, share out the handful of lemon drops that Dean had stored in his pocket, then guzzle some water and put behind us the ten pitches that remained between us and the top.

Hungry but buzzing with an urgency to reach the summit, we swarmed up the steepest thousand feet of the Nose. By late afternoon on this third day we were moving up the last pitch. Ironically, on the first ascent Harding had led this pitch in the dead of night. As I climbed up this overhanging sea of rock, I marveled at the tenacity of this gritty fellow who was something of a shadow around the climber's hangouts in Yosemite. Like us, Harding had felt the pressure to escape the wall, but he had been on it far longer than we had—twelve days on his final foray. In his book, he describes his final fourteen hours by headlamp, painfully hand drilling the twenty-eight bolts that ascend the final overhanging headwall, and from which I now hung: "By this time The Nose had really gotten to me. This thing had completely dominated my life for over a year . . . I was rather frazzled," were his words.

"Frazzled" certainly described our condition as we each popped over the rim of El Cap. We were hungry, thirsty, and bone-tired. As I peered over the rim one last time before stepping onto the flat granite slabs on top, I took note of the lay of the valley from this grand perspective. The cliffs and the roads and the meadows sprawled below me, with Half Dome and the bare granite backbone of the High Sierra curling around the horizon. It was if I were seeing Yosemite through a fisheye lens. It was a view I felt comfortable with, and it was a view I would see again, many times. Though I did not know it that day in 1979, by the end of the millennium I would make seven more ascents of this route.

Chapter 7

Big-Wall Thrills

The key to climbing well is to climb as much as you can. In Yosemite in the early 1980s, we indulged ourselves in climbing as if it were more than a full-time job. We worked at it five days a week, eight hours a day, and we put in a lot of overtime. The only problem was that the job of climbing was a job without pay. So the climbers there lived on the cheap, stretching the meager funds they accumulated during stints of seasonal employment as waitpersons, carpenters, smoke jumpers, maids, pizza deliverers, bicycle messengers, fishermen, gardeners, landscapers, concrete workers, roofers, shop assistants, ski patrollers, and every other short-term job there is. I managed to live in Camp Four for an entire summer on $75. Others lived there much longer on nearly nothing at all. To survive a climbing season in Yosemite—through the rains of spring, the heat of summer, the bliss of fall—you had to live by your wits.

The cash crop of Yosemite was the aluminum soda pop and beer cans that could be redeemed for a nickel each at the Yosemite recycling site. Tourists too impatient to harvest the five-cent value of the cans tossed an astonishing mass of beverage containers into the trash system of Yosemite. The orchards for this crop were the bearproof garbage cans and dumpsters dotted around the valley. Climbers were the fruit pickers. A meager living could be had from this.

I first learned about canning for profit when I encountered a scruffy Australian and his even scruffier British accomplice in a picnic area, pushing up the heavy lid of a dumpster and wedging a log under the lid to keep it open. As I watched, the Australian crawled into the huge steel trash bin and began noisily rummaging around, tossing cans out to the Brit, who gathered them into a shopping bag.

"What are you guys doing?" I asked.

"Existing," the Englishman said. He introduced himself as Tom, then he added that they were saving the cans from the landfills of Fresno, and saving America's environment while they were at it.

When the Aussie exited the dumpster, accompanied by a swarm of flies and yellow jackets, a family picnicking nearby and looking on with nothing resembling approval gathered up their lunch and left. The dumpster-diver introduced himself as Greg and explained that he and Tom were heading up El Cap as soon as they raised enough money to buy a new rope. They counted out the sticky cans they had foraged and told me that they had, this past week, gathered about eight hundred cans, the bulk of which were stashed in a cave behind Camp Four.

"A rope costs fifty bucks, so that means we need about two hundred more cans. Looks like another day of canning," the Aussie told his partner. Then the pair dived into the nearby Merced River, washed off the filth of their labors, and headed off.

Scarfing was another climber subsidy. It took place in the cafeteria and, like canning, was based on the fact that Yosemite tourists toss away most of what they buy. In a typical scarfing session a table of climbers would sit around drinking 25-cent cups of coffee and cramming themselves full of chemical-laden soup crackers and relish packets from the condiments counter, awaiting the next busload of tourists.

With trays weighed down by more food than they could eat, the tourists would pick at their macaroni salads, their scrambled eggs, or their french fries or whatever, until the bus driver honked the horn and the tourists fled, abandoning a bounty of half-eaten dishes. Swooping in like vultures, the climbers would grab the leftovers. The best tourists back then were the Japanese, whose robust national economy in the 1980s seemed to dictate that they should buy twice as much food as they could eat. Occasionally, scarfing led to errors in judgment. I watched Dale Bard, one of the fittest of the Yosemite climbers—he had climbed El Cap by scores of routes—intercept a tourist's half-eaten plate of bacon and eggs the moment the man left his seat at the cafeteria. Alas, the tourist had not abandoned his breakfast, he had only gone to the bathroom for a minute, and when he returned he was shocked to see Dale downing the last bite of his meal.

Avoiding campsite fees was another trick among valley regulars, and this was best accomplished by getting a berth on the Rescue Site in Camp Four. The Yosemite Search and Rescue Team was (and remains today) a loose-knit crew of climbers recruited by the National Park Service to perform high-angle cliff rescues. Free camping and minimum wages were the reward for risking your neck to save tourists lost on hiking trails or to remove injured climbers from cliffs. It was also just plain cool to be on the Rescue Team. Jim Bridwell, whether officially or simply by virtue of being the alpha male of the valley, seemed to be the chief of the Rescue Site, where he lived in a Bedouin-style tent that was party central. Under his watch the Rescue Site had also become a training zone. There was a pull-up bar tied to the fork of a tree, a rope ladder made with sections of PVC pipe, free weights lying about on a remnant of carpet, and a chain strung between two trees on which one could practice tightrope-walking—all useful tools for developing the strength and balance needed for Yosemite's climbs.

When I arrived in Camp Four, I claimed a piece of dirt covered in soft pine needles on which I could lay out my sleeping bag at night, as I had no tent, and I stored my few belongings in one of the bearproof, padlocked steel lockers in the camp. We called these heavy containers "coffins," due to their shape, and they were there to protect campers' food and gear from marauding bears. These hulking animals would steal anything resembling food and drag it into the woods, where they'd tear it apart and eat it. Littering the forest around Camp Four were shredded rucksacks that had once contained groceries, as well as toothmark-pocked cans and boxes. The bears ate anything that humans tried to hide from them, including containers of washing detergent, bars of soap, even whole tins of ground pepper.

This gypsylike lifestyle was all for a purpose: to climb for as long as possible on as little money as possible. By 1980 I felt an urge to climb that was insistent and compelling. If I could remain in Yosemite a little longer and accomplish a few more climbs by living cheap and dirty, then the means justified the end. Money and work were of little importance to us then, but money was, ironically, also the key to the climbing life. Years later, one climbing writer, Pat Ament, described me in those days as "a Chaplinesque, dirty-faced hobo of the Yosemite climbers' camp." For a few months of the year, this was true. These dirt-poor days were

Leading the famous Serenity Crack in Yosemite at age sixteen. (CHARLIE ROW)

among the best and the most carefree of my life, and though my friends were often scoundrels, I felt their friendship convincingly. Shoplifting, dining and dashing, siphoning gas, and other infractions in the name of furthering one's climbing dollars were common follies among some of the people to whom I trusted my life when I tied myself into a rope. Some of them, two decades later, are lawyers, doctors, and contractors, yet back then they were barely distinguishable from petty crooks.

Though I drew the line at stealing, I have often wondered what I would have done had I been faced with Yosemite's greatest free-money scam: the plane crash of 1977 when climbers salvaged a fortune in marijuana from a smuggler's plane that went down in the high country above Yosemite Valley. I envied the new racks of gear, the shiny new VW vans, the long and well-fed climbing road trips that a few climbers enjoyed from the fruits of that illegal salvage operation. But I also saw its dark side.

The strong odor of the "Lockheed Lodestar" weed, as Yosemite-ites called the marijuana that came from that plane, could be smelled even two years after the crash, as locals and visitors were still lighting up stashes of the mind-altering herb. According to a mix of fact and legend, the plane had, that February of '77, been sitting on a tarmac somewhere in Mexico, fueled to go, stuffed with 240 forty-pound bales of high-grade, red-haired marijuana. Its destination was some secret landing zone in the desert of California or Nevada. A shoot-out, some say, put the plane in the hands of rival drug traffickers, and the hijacked Lockheed Lodestar took off on its ill-fated flight.

Maybe the hijackers weren't savvy to the game of flying low over the contours of the land to elude U.S. radar, or maybe the owners of the cargo were so torched by the hijacking that they ratted on their own plane to the Drug Enforcement Agency. Either way, a high-speed pursuit plane intercepted the intruder and trailed it through southern California, ordering to it to change course, land, and be arrested. The pilots of the Lodestar freaked out. They flew deep into the High Sierra, far from roads or towns, running their fuel tanks low. Below them a deep winter snowpack clung to the mountains. As the plane's engines sputtered on vapors, they spotted a flat, white circle below them: Upper Merced Lake, sixteen miles as the crow flies from Yosemite Valley. The lake was frozen over with a two-foot-thick skin of ice.

In desperate straits now, the pilots lowered the undercarriage, eased the plane onto the lake, bounced once, then the ice cracked. The Lodestar augured in, the fuselage snapped in half, bales of weed spilled across the lake. The tail section containing most of the cargo sank, while the cockpit settled half-submerged into a crater of smashed ice, nose-pointing skyward. The pilots lay dead, still strapped to their seats. Soon after, during a window between snowstorms, a helicopter flight by the authorities spotted the wreck but deemed it inaccessible and conditions too cold and dangerous to venture into it, so a recovery mission was postponed until the spring thaw.

Story has it that word reached climbers' ears one rainy day when a few Camp Four regulars made a social call to a Park Service ranger's office. While they were indulging in a bit of small talk, the radio blurted out a report about the unidentified plane plowing into Upper Merced Lake. The climbers asked a few questions and learned that no cops or rangers would be heading up there until spring. Only one of the climbers who'd heard this news had the gumption to suit up in his winter clothes, clip on his beat-up cross-country skis, and head into the backcountry for a look. The others feared they'd get into trouble. But when their friend returned a few days later with a heavy backpack full of weed, the lure of easy money drew the rest of them up to the lake.

What happened next is tainted by the retelling of a hundred people who were not there and by the secrecy of the handful who were, but by the end of a few more days several Yosemite climbers were rich. Climbers zeroed in on the plane crash while authorities put off the recuperation efforts, mainly because the climbers thought nothing of trudging all day through thigh-deep snow to reach their destination. The survival instincts required by winter camping and the toughness to put up with being wet and cold for days on end is second nature to a lot of climbers, but, evidently, it was unthinkable to the DEA, FBI, and Park Service folk.

The first climbers to reach the wreck found easy pickings, and harvested the bales off the top of the frozen lake. Stunned by their luck, they instantly realized that the value of one bale of weed far surpassed the cost of their winter camping gear, so they dumped everything out of their packs and crammed them full of weed. Conveniently, the bales fitted neatly into a rucksack. As more climbers visited the lake, the